Love ReWorked

Love, Sex, & Relationships

Re-Forming, Re-Presenting, & Re-Approaching

Darrell L. Owens

To Deztiny & Kelsie,

Thanks for the love!

God Bless D. Ow—

DEDICATION

I dedicate this book to my parents, Bishop D. Lee Owens and Lady Edna M. Owens. Who taught me to think for myself and to love myself. They gave me the self-esteem to rise and stand out from the status quo. They introduced me to God then gave me back to him to serve others. Mama I could never pay you or daddy back for your sacrifice and love towards me. You are everything in God and I love you!

To my friends, supporter, and partners, you motivate me, and push me to be exceptional. Thank you.

To the teachers, mentors, pastors, activist, public intellectuals, scholars, and philosophers that have inspired me to be a truth teller and have demonstrated the virtue in choosing truth over personal gain. Most of which will never know their impact on my journey, I am eternally grateful. You taught me how to live exceptionally.

To all of my immediate family, thank you all, for undergirding my passion and drive. Without you there is no me. Especially my sisters and my bro. of whom I owe tremendous gratitude and thanks. To my beautiful children, I am extremely proud of you and I love you, but remember that love loves you the most.

To my beloved church and spiritual children, thank you for allowing me the privilege of covering your existence. You validate my calling, my ministry, and this work.

CONTENTS

Love ReWorked

Exceptional Love 9

Love Me Before You Like Me 16

Battle Of The Sexes 22

Body Heat (Attraction) 29

Finding Romance in The Modern Day 38

Friendship 45

Sex ReWorked

I Just Want To See You Strip 54

Sex In The Bible 59

Pre-Marital Sex & Fornication 73

Masturbation 95

Dating ReWorked

Why People Lie & Cheat 105

The Principle of "So Far" 113

Best Practices For a Healthy Relationship 117

CONTENTS CONT.

Rejecting Manipulation 122

4 Potential Placements For The People Who 129
Come Into Your Life

5 Ways to Get a Good Man and Keep Him 133

5 Ways to Get a Good Woman and Keep Her 138

Dating Wisdom For Those 25 and Younger 141

Marriage ReWorked

The Madness of Marriage 154

The Confusion of a Beautiful Covenant 163

Biblical Marriage VS Traditional Marriage 171

The Genius of The Mistress 181

He That Finds a Wife, Made Right 193

Understanding Divorce 197

ReWorked Principles for Marriage 213

The Inspiration for Love ReWorked 225

Biography 226

Preface

The concept of reworking basically teaches us that the point is still the point regardless of the particular method of a thing. Reworking teaches us that models, methods, and practices can be improved and made better. In every discipline and in every generation you will find customization and improvement. It is inspired by individual exceptionalism, accumulated knowledge, and modern culture. We should all be very skeptical of any one who is *are* unfriendly towards new ideas that reform or improve process and results! The idea that we should refer to a time past as the central guide to going forward is not helpful and is counterproductive. People don't want the original cell phone, they don't want the original computers designed, and they certainly don't want a washboard rather than their washing machines! Jesus said, "old skins can not handle the vitality of the new wine, if you force this union it will destroy both the old and the new!" We have a religious culture that has a bad tendency to regard going backwards rather than going forward!

At one time music was produced on reel-to-reels this was exciting but then came along the phonic record, then the cassette tape and ultimately the CD. All the while music was still the point even though the method and model of how we get music changed drastically the point is still the same! This book is far from an exhaustive manual on how to navigate the wide range of intimate relationships that we all engage in but it is an introduction to a completely new approach to any relationship. Check any major bookstore for the section of books on love, dating, or relating to the opposite sex or any sex for that matter and you will find little to know resources for becoming informed. When they take you to the section even close to what you're looking for you will find lots of books on sex and a ton on marriage but almost nothing at all on successful intimate connection or relationship! Love ReWorked was written to help you think differently about love, sex, and relationships. To help you observe human behavior, learn the lessons that it teaches, and to help you get comfortable with relating to intimate love interest without; fear, manipulation, or obsessing.

It is my belief that the attempt to connect with others in an intimate relationship should not leave us victimized. While relationships do require effort and sacrifice, they should not feel like a chore nor should they come at the expense of our future potential, or our dreams! This book is my deliberate attempt to make you conscious of the power of love to help you have a healthy relationship. If we as individuals are going to ever walk in unity with one another, there must be a decline in the human influence from the outside of our relationships, and there must be an increase in our dependence on love's ability to love us within it. If we can give individuals room to express themselves and to experience one another through the exceptional gift of love we all will experience greater success. It is my hope that after reading this book you will walk away inspired by love as God created it, not as men have defined it! That you would not hide your dysfunction or discontent with love, sex and relationships but finally live happily ever after.

Exceptional Love

How you define love in modern culture will have a very powerful effect on your success in love relationships. It is important not to bog love down with broken images, distorted definitions, and passed along religious assumptions. Love reworked is a way we can understand and re-present love more accurately and more constructively. It is a path to exceptional love, a love that can literally change your life! It is my absolute conviction that love speaks, love teaches, and that love, loves us all the most! This love has no desire to judge us, and no need to change us essentially! This is exceptional love, it is perfect and constant, it is generous and unrestrictive. Exceptional love defines "itself" in your reality and in our modern culture. This love transcends the simple translations of a few Greek words. The Greek word Phileo means, brotherly concern or friendship, this is not love, its friendship.

The Greek word Storge (stor-gae) means, family friendship or family connection, this is not love, its friendship and affection within the family. The Greek word Eros means, sensuality or to arouse sexually, this is not love, its physical pleasure. The Greek word Agape historically had no particular religious connotation at all. It was an ancient classic Greek word used to express all of the previously list words above at one time. It was Christians that changed the definition of Agape and used it to express what they call the highest form of love, which is the love of God. Agape is a literal translation of the word love, however it does not define love at all. This exceptional love I'm speaking of is not sex, if it were the only requirement necessary for loving a person would be to have sex with them. This love is not a feeling, if it were it would be right to fall in and out of love, weekly even daily! Love is not desire, if it were it would be fine not to love anyone or anything you don't have any passion for!

When we define love in these ways we cause disturbance and unrest in our worlds at the level of consciousness! These definitions of love are misleading and based on religious assumptions passed along because we are blind, careless and at this point negligent! These definitions of love are the kinds of love spoken of, and written about by secular poets in our culture a/k/a artist. However, these definitions do us all a great disservice. For the record it is possible to talk about sex, passion, and connection without confusing them with love! Exceptional love is an evolved, profound, and cosmic love that must be revealed and caught by the heart and the consciousness. Exceptional love is not new; the culture is just more conscious of it and it's importance for our existence than ever before. This awakening to love and its affect enables us to see another's truth and accept it without a need to alter it or to manipulate it for one's own purposes! Some may feel that this kind of love allows people to get away with their dirt and that it let's them act any way they want to, but this is far from the truth.

This love is not passive or inactive it understands human process, it supports and cooperates with others as they grow and evolve each day. This love is very effective in growing and guiding the soul through the deep waters of life. It is love's assignment to guard, defend, and to secure our hearts and our peace. What love gives to us doesn't come from the intellect, or the voices, nor the facts on the peripheral of our lives. Love goes far beyond them and presents us truth like only love can. The mission of exceptional love is to introduce peace and safety to all human connections, not just our sexual one's or the connections that end in matrimony. This love provides this peace for anyone who will allow love to bring them truth, wisdom, and spiritual direction without any partiality or discrimination. If exceptional love is not present in your consciousness and your heart, judgment will flow through everything you do. It will flow through your touch, your point of view, and your words. It will affect your ability to trust and the way you handle those who attempt to genuinely connect with you. Love is the way to experience a person safely, intimately, and with dignity.

Love ReWorked

When we walk in judgment rather than love we are more destructive than we know. We become an emotional menace to everyone we are connected to, destroying their peace and emotional health then ultimately we turn on ourselves becoming self-destructive. When we are fearful and judgmental we cause damage and then re-produce after our own kind in the lives of the victims of our judgment creating a vicious cycle of ruin. The amount of damage that "judgment" creates cannot be measured it is immense! Show me a judgmental person and I'll show you a person who has been judged! Show me a hurtful person and I will show you a person who has been deeply hurt! Consequently many people walk around playing the role of a peaceful person or the role of a confident individual trying not to expose the truth that they are broken and fearful. This vicious cycle has created a generation of men and women who live emotionally guarded and with fragile mental states that at the slightest challenge or trouble in relationship they assume a position of defense. Defending against the pain of being judged.

So now we have a lot of broken and fearful people who have been judged, now judging others which only drives the others with their dysfunctions into hiding, and underground. Only for these dysfunctions to resurface and disrupt all new attempts to be healthy and happy. Exceptional love is the remedy for both those who have been judged and those who carry a judgmental heart. This love evicts fear and prepares men and women to genuinely connect with others. This love unfolds the emotional and guarded arms of the soul allowing us to connect to new opportunities and people without us ruining a potential relationship before it can even have a chance. Exceptional love changes the game and gives every individual the chance to be healed and to improve their ability to connect with others in love relationships. This book is my way of introducing us to that love. Love is the "Great Human Equalizer" it reveals truth and gives direction to our humanity. It gives us the capacity to know truth and the grace to bear that truth even when it isn't what we hoped it would be. This love is the cosmic and divine energy of God that causes us to acknowledge all truth, affirm all people, and to accept all as they are!

We need love; it enables us to bear the truth about both our own and other's strengths and weaknesses. Exceptional love takes away the fear of heartbreak and disappointment, if you let it live in your consciousness. It sets the stage for two people in a relationship to experience connection, romance, and ecstasy. So I present to some and introduce to others exceptional love. I pray that your heart will become conscious of exceptional love, and that you experience the extraordinary!

Darrell L. Owens

Love Me Before You Like Me

It almost never fails, you meet somebody really nice, they're sweet and very endearing, and they fascinate you. Your mind snaps an image of that person in a single moment, in time, and there you have it, you say to yourself, "I think I may be falling in love with them." You have one dinner, take one stroll, and see one outfit and said, damn, sign me up! Not realizing you could be signing up for, Heartbreak! In a single moment you've been captivated by an image of a person that is not complete. An image created by the endorphins in your brain that produce a sense of well being, and a strong sense of pleasure that could only be topped by an orgasm. In one moment and sometime in a compilation of moments, you start making serious choices about intimacy based off of insufficient knowledge about that person. This all happens lightening fast in that moment and you buy it, you start buying into the image before you really know the person's truth! You say to your self, "If there's more I'll find out later, but right now, please don't kill my vibe."

Then you rush and bring them into your personal space, mix them within your safe circle, and allow them access to knowledge about you with no commitment from them for anything, just a hope. You tell yourself that everybody that loves me, is going to like them, but you yourself don't even know them! Based off of the three or four images or moments your heart has of them, your mind says, they are always sweet, and not self-serving, and always got it together. You say this to your self only for time to begin to reveal who they really are. Then you reluctantly and slowly begin to see clearly that this person is not just sweet, or just nice, or just the feeling or sense you felt in those moments. You begin to realize that there were other facts and truths that you had no clue existed. Basically you ran head first into a committed relationship without knowing the small print of the relationship. After you've given them a key to your house, access to your family and finances, signed for something in your name and made yourself completely vulnerable to them. Now they come out of the closet, now you want to cry foul, but you couldn't wait for love!

He or she cheats with the next-door neighbor but you couldn't wait for love, they persuade you to pay her bills including other family's bills but you couldn't wait for love. They lied to you repeatedly, they've humiliated you in front of those that care for you most but you couldn't wait for love. Now your singing that familiar song "tell me the truth", "Tell me the Truth", "TELL ME THE FU*KING TRUTH"! All along love had so much to say but you couldn't wait for love. Now your complaint is, "I didn't deserve this," "I'm a good person," and "I was good to you, why can't you be good to me?" "They're not playing fair." Here you are begging an insensitive and potentially dysfunctional person to be a father or your mother and pat you up because your feelings are hurt and you are ashamed and lost. Here's the wisdom, **"Love Them before You Like Them"**. When you meet someone, if they are on drugs you might not like them but you have to love them. If a person turns out to be a liar, you might not like them but you have to love them. If they only want to use you and not really be with you, you might not like them but you have to still love them.

Reworked cosmic love doesn't have any exceptions or groups of people considered unlovable. Loving people before you like them allows people to be good or bad, it allows them to be strong or weak it doesn't have a preference, it is completely willing to "cooperate" with what is. This love changes the odds and changes the testimony of your life. Love is the great equalizer and power that causes us to detect and know truth. It is the fearlessness that causes us to embrace others and their truth as it is and not as we hope for it to be. Love is the energy that takes us to the next step past getting to know a person on to perceiving their indefinite truth beneath the surface. While others may try to love you, believe it or not, love loves you the most! The truth is when we initially say we like someone we are speaking from a limited view of the person's complete truth. Love on the other hand reveals those truths continuously and gives us the insight to really assess and know the person and their truth we say we like. Love is like a personal mechanic who checks out a used car before you purchase it. The mechanic is there to see what you can't see. They protect you from making a bad decision or a regrettable one.

And you trust them to tell you the truth. Well the same applies to love in life. Love will help you to choose the right person to date or the right partner to marry. It will serve to protect you from making a bad decision or a regrettable one. It will show you what you cannot see on the surface. This is not an attempt to rob life of its mystery this is you and I using the divine, cosmic energy known as love to experience happiness. You shouldn't live your life always saying, "If I Knew then, what I know now". Love has always had something to say, if you would ever listen to it. If you have ever tried to be in love according to society and culture's definitions, one thing you realize very quickly is that people are not very good at revealing their private truth. Some people have very sensible reasons for this and others obviously are malicious in intent, but generally speaking, it is not plausible or realistic that people would reveal all their private truth. Understand that a person can only reveal what they are conscious of and can currently remember. The fact of the matter is; we are not continuously and fully aware of all of the motives and intents of our hearts minute-to-minute, or experience-to-experience.

This would require us to be conscious of all the immediate happenings around us and to be conscious of what is happening in our sub-consciousness. This would take an extraordinary shift in human consciousness and perception to be even plausible. The only real probable way to experiencing a safe and healthy relationship with others is to have a authentic connection to love and the insight that it brings! People can hide from you but they can't hide from love! Love should be your closest confidant, your soul's mate, your source and resource, drink from it until you are filled. With, understanding, clarity, and direction. Take love's counsel to heart and let it pass over your soul like the sun rising in the wake of the morning. Let it establish your footing so you have no cause to be afraid. Open your ear and hear love's whisper and let it be your inside trader, guiding you on the journey as you traverse through what people say out of their mouths verses the actual intent of their hearts. Let love anchor you so that if a person attacks your heart and means you no good, you can remain standing, safe and stable. *Love Works, when love has been Reworked!*

Darrell L. Owens

Battle Of The Sexes

The goal of love relationships seems simple. We all want to be happy and embraced by others hoping to share our lives and its joys with someone that feels the same about us. It seems that love relationships consist of a lot of meaningless sex, dysfunction, and disappointment! It seems to be very little happiness and intimate construction. These familiar sentiments about love and relationships can be transformed through understanding. Understanding makes the difference and changes how you act and react. If I walk into a shoe store and I find a pair of shoes that I have been searching for forever and I purchase the shoes and get all the way home only to find when I open the box a large mark and scratch down the side of one of the shoes, how I act and react is going to be vastly different if when I go to buy the shoes the salesman shows me the scratch and helps me understand the circumstances of what I'm buying and I purchase them anyways. Then it would be absurd for me to act or react the same way, as if I didn't know?

The problem with love relationships is there are a lot of people marrying, a lot of people having sex, but not a lot of understanding. When you think about dysfunction in love relationships, most people have a better relationship with there cell phone! You care more about where it is and if its ok, you cover it and coddle it. You're especially careful not to drop it! When it struggles to make the connection you wait for it and walk with until it gets better. Even the commercials about your cell phone sound like some new elite dating service telling you they have found the right one for you! Yet the people in our lives we say we love and hold dear, we handle them with a great deal more neglect, it is quite interesting to watch this play out in our society. This observation begs the question, can we only be happy as long as others do things our way and do what we want them to do? I find this to be true in both men and women the only difference is the time lines. Women generally wait until they're partner makes the relationship exclusive then she will demonstrate this kind of mistreatment. While men tend to show this abuse initially and up front. So ensues the "Battle Of The Sexes"!

The truth of what you're dealing with when it comes to the battles of the sexes is, a whole lot of people really "don't understand" what it means to be in a mutually loving, sacrificial, and intimate relationship. What many men and women expect from their love relationship is the same kind relationship they have with their mother or fathers just add sex! I know that was tough to hear but suffer me for one moment longer. Think about it, there is nothing mutual about your relationship with your parents by way of love or sacrifice, and there is no sexual intimacy at all. Starting off your parents by and large see themselves as your foundation, your launching pad and responsible to supply your needs and as many of your personal desires as possible. It is thankless and they expect nothing in return except respect. This is in the hope you will succeed! Their commitment to you is far greater than yours to them for an extended period of time and they gladly accept it. In fact they welcome it! Think about this carefully, this is the context of what you are accustomed to!

You expect and damn near demand to be treated like this from anybody who says they love you; pastor, teacher, friend, and Co-workers because when you hear "I love you" you instantly refer to your parent's love which sums up your idea of how it is supposed to be if you say you love me! Without a second thought and with a clear conscience if a person says they love you, (you immediately think mommy/daddy) If they ask you for, or offer you mutual love and respect, you think to yourself, then you say it out loud, "You Don't Love Me!" because if you did you'd take care of me, and let me have my way and get away with not paying for myself or being responsible for myself, you don't love me! Think about it, they only asked you for the basics of being in a mutually loving, sacrificial, intimate relationship. This is a realistic expectation and request, but it turns into a fight with you! This is the attitude going in the door with most people, and this is all happening internally long before great sex and the tides of emotion have even began to flow. Then accusations made of not being loved by someone who wants to be your mate and not your parent spins from a misunderstanding, to a fight, to a battle and from a battle to an all out war!

The World Wide Web and what we know, as the Internet is basically a network of networks. Private, public, academic, business, and government all linked by a broad array of "optical wireless technologies." Even now it's breathtaking to have the ability to resource from millions of different specialist, disciplines, and forums from wherever you are in the world! This is the beauty of the Internet. In a tangible way we can see, regardless of language, culture, or geographic location every network uses the same stuff for "connectivity"! So it is with love relationships men and women both use the exact same stuff for connectivity! Basically we all need attention, desire, acceptance, companionship, and trust in order to be happy and healthy. When I say "basically," I'm saying these are essential, the minimum required and they foundationally support everything else relationships bring! Like marriage; children, adversity, and the fulfillment of dreams. When I say we all "need" these things, we need them like the car needs gas, like your brain needs oxygen, and the earth needs rain, we need them! To be without them renders all off us male or female too dysfunctional to remain happy in anybody's life.

The challenging thing is, we live in a "Google Chrome" society, so it is far easier to stay distracted from reality and to explore new ways to pacify the people we say we love rather than to satisfy them by meeting their relational needs. So he keeps giving her expensive dinners, shopping sprees, and Viagra nights but all she wants is his attention. She keeps showing him those pole classes paid off and how freaky she can get but all he wants is validation. Sex is not enough glue to hold a relationship together! So don't be fooled by the myth they call a battle between the sexes, it is not a battle, it is confusion! Confusion created by lack of understanding the difference in being satisfied verses being pacified. Confusion based on age-old assumptions about the opposite sex passed down to our detriment! Keeping all this in mind there is such a thing as real genuine happiness to be found in a balanced, mutually loving relationship! This happiness requires understanding to be enjoyed. Understanding gives both the man and the woman the ability to overcome what we know as the "Battle Of The Sexes" The first great blessing of understanding is that it disarms confusion and over-reaction!

Ignorance and misconception about intimate love and how men and women relate to one another is what instigates the myth of the "Battle of the Sexes". Yes, I believe it is a myth, false evidence appearing real, it is the crown jewel of ignorance, mistaking lust for love! I say this because the sexes are more alike than they are different. Besides a gynecologist there is no female brain doctor or a male eye doctor, and when it comes to relationship and love the same holds true. We are more alike than we are different. People walk through relational experiences and are profoundly changed and many times damaged? The cure and prescription is, understanding. Fortunately, the strategy to get this understanding, is Love ReWorked and your holding it!

Body Heat (Attraction)

Attraction is the trait within you that desires connection with others. You desire his or her attention, their touch and their general presence. However, attraction oftentimes is based off of shallow facts about people that distract you from the realities of who they are at their core. People are not good at hiding those realities. We are just great at ignoring them. Especially when those realities are not what we want them to be! Like an addict we pursue people off of the sensations on the surface and the euphoria of new conquest. This is called body heat. That sense of attraction that causes us to disregard the signs of other's true character even when they expose themselves. We get completely obsessed with the external rather than the internal character of the people we are attracted to. This creates the illusion of value and significance. To be caught by an illusion is a dreadful thing. Like the illusion of there being, "a type." Seeking a "type" of person is one of the central illusions and reasons women and men whined up dicked dumb and pussy whipped!

These maxims accurately depict the condition and mindset of people with bad information with bad thinking who cut bad deals they call relationships. They represent when we are not thinking straight or with clarity. When seeking companionship you should watch out for the idea of a particular "type" and stop using the term "my type" when seeking and engaging in courtship. The poet Jamie Foxx said it all to well, "I swear I always fall for your type." This was a poetic lament about being attracted to what is initial, obvious and on the surface, but ultimately finding what's not good for you at the core! Be careful using surface, generic, and "positive characteristics" to decide if someone is right for you. Everybody wants someone honest, caring, and faithful, with a sense of humor, groomed, with character, spiritual, and good looking. So if this is what you call "My Type" duh, we get it, but all of these things must be time tested under pressure! Anybody can be awesome in a moment of time, but who are they and what do they really want at their core! You have to replace the idea of having a particular "type" with desire for what is "true and right".

We spend our teenaged years falling into puppy love, we get to our twenties and we are deranged and in love, in our thirties and we're madly in love, but by the time we hit our late forties we wake up, and all of the foolishness about, "not my type" goes out the window. At this point we brake down and just say, "I don't have a list," "I don't have any special request and there are no prerequisites," "I just want what's RIGHT for me!" The idea that there's a particular type of man or woman that will make you happy is misleading and a mistake! All of this misdirection plays off of your attraction to the surface knowledge of who people are. This kind of thinking makes you think you can judge and understand who a person is through a few shallow experiences a couple of appearances of good character and even fewer facts, and this is just not so! Attraction is the fruit of your feelings. We are attracted to what brings us pleasure or feels right to us. However, your feelings don't possess enough insight or information alone to make sound decisions for your life and guide it into the right direction!

Feelings are the "children" of our self-consciousness; you don't let your children operate in areas beyond their capacity or in dangerous places. You put your children in a safe place to play; you should put your feelings in a safe place to feel! No matter how good a person makes you feel, it is irresponsible to just turn on the autopilot and hope for the best in intimate relationships! You are risking the most valued treasure you posses in the world, your heart! Don't give your feelings control over your discernment or your decisions. Your feelings alone don't have the ability to make proper decisions for your life. If you fail to manage these "children" of your self-consciousness (feelings) they will break your heart! Think about the moth, the moth does not discriminate as to what kind of light it's attracted too it just goes in the direction of the light it sees. When you see a person's public persona, their talents, and a flash of their greatness that's the light and you're just going in the direction of their light. But you need to know who they really are beneath the surface and beyond the body heat! The light you see could be a campfire or it could be a wildfire. If it's a campfire at their core, this can be productive and beneficial.

However if it's a wildfire at their core this will threaten any possible relationship and intimate connection! So look into the people you're connecting with until things are clear, because like the moth you may see the light and be attracted to it but you need to know what type of light your headed into. The great part is, you have something the moth doesn't have, love! We on the other hand spend laborious amounts of time seeking the recipe that will attract the right person into our lives almost as if potential love interests are like animals to be caught by the skill of a hunter. We assume we can make others meet our needs and be what we envision them to be. But people are very complex with many layers and there is more to them than what meets the eye! You have to be careful not to attract people by holding yourself out with a persona or principles that don't represent who you really are! Men attach their worth to money; clothes, and cars, women tie their worth to purses and clothes and to how much of a freak they can be! We hold these things out as, "Who We Are" but you are not your money, you are not your car, you are not how much of a freak you can be!

The person you're going to find true love with and "fall in love with" does not care about what's on the surface. They desire the real you and your truth. You have to accept and celebrate your truth even in the midst of rejection or disappointment! Your truth is the best attraction for others, they can't deny your truth and nor can you. This becomes the magnetism that draws the right person to you. You have to do things that are true and not the things you think will cause other people to approve of, or desire you. All this is not to say that economic and social fluency are wrong or irrelevant to intimate love relationships. Or to say that one's physical appearance is not important. On the contrary it is important that no matter what your style or flow is, it should be genuine and reflect pride! I'm saying that surface issues should not be the guiding factors or bases for happiness or longevity in a relationship. Time and experience has proven to us that, people can experience deep attractions to one another initially. This is known as infatuation or body heat. Infatuation is attraction that is intense and impressionable, but it is short lived and fleeting. Every relationship that starts with infatuation must experience a shift and rest on the character of the individuals involved?

If this does not happen, "it will not last!" When a relationship is based on external, shallow, and temporary facts like the body or the bank account it is doomed! Inevitably no matter how infatuated you are with another person's external presence, at some point everyone's external will go from amazing to basic. We all at some point start looking further and deeper for something more beneath the surface. We start looking for strength and credibility. You hear often that people are attracted to what they see, smell, and everything external first. I want you to be very cautious because this can be "short sighted" and misleading! It is problematic when we endeavor to judge people based on the external and ignore the internal substantive parts! Attraction misunderstood can turn into the fire of lust. Lust is an irreverent energy within the soul. It is a legitimate attempt to meet legitimate needs and desires through illegitimate means. Lust is your attempt to meet your human and spiritual needs outside of true love. Your spirituality, sexuality, and sensuality often times get crossed up.

It is spiritually plausible that you can be experiencing a spiritual need but engage in sexual or your sensual resources. It is sexually plausible that you can be experiencing a sexual need but engage in spiritual or your sensual resources. Both scenarios leave you with; dissatisfaction and exploring illegitimate means to satisfy your legitimate needs! Lust causes people to act out of character in desperate attempts to get what they want. Often what people want in these instances are they're basic human intangible needs met! Lust causes you to miss the important things an to be preoccupied with urgent things, this doesn't allow you to read the small print of what it cost you for moving so fast and blindly. Lust let's you commit to a relationship with a person without all the essential things you need to endure all the test you will face in that relationship. Lust gets you into a marriage but leaves you too broken, insecure and unwise to manage it or deserve it! Lust will make you have sex with, and mess over someone who wasn't supposed to be a sex partner, but was to be a true friend for your entire life! Lust will cause you to seek to become pregnant or to get someone pregnant in order to control their free will and their desire to be or not be with you!

You must be careful not to want something more than you want it right. Once your attraction has turned into lust without true love being present, all involved in the relationship are in danger! If you want to attract the right people into your life be busy doing what you are good at and with what interest you. You want to be found engaged in these things because; they reveal who you are, why you are, and where you want to go! People in these settings get to experience your character, greatness and strength! So be encouraged, the problems in our lives are not created because of our attraction or the fact that we have desires; the trouble comes when we fail to engage in exceptional love and wisdom when we find ourselves attracted to others. We know that sex is not enough glue to hold a relationship together. We know that an amazing body is not enough to keep a man's attention and money can't make someone be loyal to you! Don't try to pray away your passions, desires, or your sense of attraction. Allow love to teach you to be self-aware and relationally-aware of all the dynamics of your interactions with those you feel attracted to!

Darrell L. Owens

Finding Romance In The Modern Day

My father, the late Bishop D. Lee. Owens would say, "don't
make people glad twice, glad you came and glad you're gone!"
This mantra is very appropriate for love relationships! When you
meet someone and they agree to go out with you this is a very
crucial moment in any relationship and most people handle it
completely wrong. They are extremely careless because it is the
beginning. There are no strikes, no drama, no pressure, and no
debt just potential. However, this moment is where 75% percent
of most relationships are lost. If someone agrees to go on a date
with you it says, at least they are open to the potential of who
you may be in their life. It says they're open to what this could
be and it suggest maybe "you could be the one," perhaps true
love for them. This is the time you should be talking about your
dreams and hopes, what motivates you and why? This is not the
time to be super intense, extreme or common. You just met them
less than 63 hours ago.

This is not the time to act like you're someone or something that you're not and it's not the time to whip out your list of do's and don'ts. When you do this people read you as an over-reactive, needy, and frankly, a chore of a person to deal with. Their just waiting for the buzzer to sound so they can get away from you! You have left no room for love to work in your favor. You have from the very onset begun to force and control everything including what the other person wants and how they feel. You can't make someone feel you or like you with demands and list, this is not attractive or desirable. The moral of the story is, if you overreact and misfire in the early stages of a relationship before trust and respect have been established, people will conclude that; "you are not the one", and the potential that was, will leak out and be wasted. And at the end of the night they'll just be glad twice, glad you came and glad your gone! Extremism and force sabotage romance. Romance is by nature, spontaneous and born out of environment, creativity and passion. These things can't be analyzed under a microscope, tested in a lab, or written down in a recipe they are too far reaching.

It is technology and science that gives people the sense that we can answer any question, solve every problem and take a pill for every discomfort. This mentality has carried over and retarded our ability to know love and intimacy in the form of romance. Most people rarely experience romance but even when they do, they many times don't realize it! Most people don't know what romance even is! Romance is the mysterious energy and excitement that is associated with companionship, connection, and cooperation! Romance it is the result of certain factors being present within an intimate connection! Just like hot and cold together result in steam and red and blue together result in the color purple, liberty, creativity and passion together result is romance. Romance is not the result of love. If you love someone this simply means that you accept him or her for who they are without a need to judge them or to change them. Love does not create romance. Romance causes focus; it spawns positivity, it flows into your profession, your interaction with your family, and your view of the world and life. It makes you go home and want to work on yourself more.

It will make you want to get your personal business affairs straight, because you'll want to earn the respect and trust of the person you experience this romance with. It will make you clean your house and throw old stuff away. What you are doing is preparing for the new possibilities ahead of you. It is a mysterious energy but it brings the best out of you! When you experience the energy of romance with someone even on a surface level it will make you contemplate and even move to separate from people you know are a waste of your time. Romance is not figment of your imagination so be careful with culture because it can be very deceptive making you believe that romance is only for the very wealthy or the smartest one among us or even popular cultures image of beauty. Pay attention to the affects that watching movies and listening to art can have on your psyche. These mediums can create a desire to experience something that just doesn't exist in reality! We do ourselves a disservice when we believe that art and entertainment have any merit when it comes to reality, because at some point we get confronted with the realities we have to actually deal with.

These realities sometimes painfully teach us even forcing us to realize that those images and scenarios we see and hear are contrived, pretended, and manufactured in a studio! It can be hard to keep right perspective because of the magnitude of images and their affect in and on our culture but it is a necessary challenge to be overcome! Take note of some of the parts that constitute romance.

Flirtation, flirting should always be present between potential lovers. It is fresh air of the love relationship it nurtures all the other essential elements of romance! Flirtation exercises the senses and enhances the early interactions of two people. Most people start off flirting but stop after they get acquainted and pre-mature sex cuts short a very important time in the relationship. The smile is a powerful characteristic of flirting it shows a genuine interest in a person! Teasing is also a kind of flirting it can be a little risky but when measured it can be a very effective way to flirt. Romance is also sponsored by spontaneity. This allows you to fully experience the energy and excitement of the one you are with.

Spontaneity is allowing mystery, creativity, and suspense to bond you with the person you are sharing with. Spontaneity breaks all the rules and operates off of being in the moment! The enemy of spontaneity is anticipation and rushing to ask what's next. Romance demands that we be present in the "now," to rush to the next moment tranquilizes spontaneity! In a relationship this becomes our subconscious attempt to contrive the growth and connection of the relationship. The way you offset the subconscious attempt to control the flow of the relationship is to learn to embrace the mysteries of life in general and then you can do it with your relationship. I promise it will make the experience worth it if you don't try to predict it, or over invest too early but stay present in the moment. To seek to orchestrate romance kills it before it can get started. It produces disappointment, heartbreak, and no romance at all! Ultimately, it is your exceptionalism that sets the tone for romance to be born in your relationship. You have to allow romance to emerge out of carless play and not bog it down with worry and anticipation for how it all plays out.

Be uniquely you not a bad copy of someone else. Find out what makes you interesting and different. Allow your self to be explored and, explore others, in the most racy, colorful, and lip-licking way! This way you can find romance in modern day love connections and nurture that romance for all of time!

Friendship

In my 15 years of counseling and caring for the spiritual and
emotional healing of hundreds of men and women, I believe I've
discovered the missing link to all relationships especially
intimate ones. I don't know if we have ever really realized the
unique greatness of friendship or what it offers. But friendship
provides what I call, Low Risk Interactive Training. This is
simply the way in which people learn to interact with others
fairly, firmly and faithfully. However, friendship is
misunderstood and covered in great misconception. People often
use it as a cliché and say; my love and I were "friends first." This
is the problem with most relationships right now today.
Friendship is what relationships are based on, I don't mean
between you and the one you're in relationship with should be
friends first, I'm talking about you having solid friendships
before you get to the relationship stage in life! Anyone balanced
by and engaged in true friendships will have a foundation that
will enrich all of his or her other relationships.

Especially potential intimate love relationships as they present themselves. There is almost nothing in society that doesn't provide you an opportunity to try the thing, and make mistakes that don't cost you! Love relationships are not one of those things! In love if you miss-step and turn someone off, it is extremely hard to regain they're interest or to recover the mental stimulation that once was present. This is because people tend to move on very quickly from what turns them off. The questions are; how are people supposed to develop their interpersonal skills or their personalities? When relationships are so sensitive and easy to miscarry? The answer is, go get some Friends! Friendship is the place where you have the responsibility to personally grow but not the pressure to provide pleasure and suitability! This is extremely important because it lifts so much pressure off of an individual to perform and to please someone else. Instead you are afforded the luxury of working on yourself and experiencing personal growth!

The ideal friendship that will bring the most benefit is one with the opposite sex. Friendship especially with the opposite sex will provide for you what counseling, conferences, and money cannot! This friendship is non-sexual, there are some things you can only get from true friendships that are nonsexual like free opportunities to get a lot of stuff wrong and not be penalized for them. Friendship should be based off of substance and not selfishness. In friendship you take a class on compassion, you learn not to be self-serving and how to put yourself in another's shoes before you judge. This all may sound basic but let me make my case. In friendship you take a class on sacrifice where you learn that it doesn't always have to be your way and sometimes the people in your life need you to think just about them and not about yourself that day! It teaches you how to accept being inconvenienced for someone you're in relationship with! Then it teaches you how to "feel' or sense the mood and state of mind of others. You learn how to realize the particular way a person would like to be talked to, respected, and left alone sometimes.

It would not be in your best interest to take these classes in real time with the actual person you are trying to be in (intimate) love relationship with. By the time you get through making your mistakes and smoothing out the rough spots of those lessons you should've learned at the friendship level, the person you are interested in has taken all they can take, so they quit the relationship and tap out! I can almost guarantee that you are terrible at intimate relationships if you have not successfully managed the vital stage of nonsexual friendship particularly with the opposite sex! The problem with friendships that are sexual is that they introduce impulses that color and alter the wisdom from the other person. This varies to different degrees but it is safer to exclude the emotional challenges sex presents for both the man and the woman. Sex with friends is intoxicating and has a way of impairing one's judgment. When two people are trying to have a true friendship it will come with the test of sexual attraction. It can be very challenging but it is a challenge that must be overcome. The blessing and payoff of not being sexual with solid true friends is priceless!

When a woman has an issue in her relationship, it is unfortunate that she doesn't have a strong, knowledgeable, trusted male friend to resource from or to get advice from. The same goes for men when they get together in a powwow everybody is saying what they believe but there isn't one woman involved in the conversation! Friendship is about men and women establishing a foundation at one level that will promote success at the next level. Having the opposite sex present allows men to teach and advise women, and women to teach and advise men. This is not to say that men cant speak to men about women or vice versa, it is just to say it's not done as well as with the opposite sex.

When a man meets a woman who has; sex appeal, takes care of herself; one who has ambition and a good personality, it can be extremely trying not to violate the covenant of friendship. Because the natural tendency for a man when he feels attraction is to act on it without considering everything he may be potentially compromising. Men can also get caught up with their imagination and wonder what it might be like to be with someone they have this kind of respect for.

Other times men engage women they may be attracted to sexually to feel more comfortable, because men tend to gain a sense of comfort and confidence once they have displayed their sexual prowess. Women can also misjudge the strong male figures in their lives to. When a woman finds a man that she can trust, one who has resources, who knows his way around in life, and one who seems to care selflessly for them, this can be hard for her not to want to be sexual with him. Women unfortunately are conditioned many times to prove their worth by offering access to their sex and intimacy. Culture has overtly and subliminally taught women that their worth was tied to their sexual ability. That somehow they can prove their level of commitment by fulfilling the sexual needs of the male! This is why you should never teach a young woman to use her sex and intimacy as a way to get something she wants, like marriage! In these moments both the male and the female are mislead and are attempting to fulfill legitimate needs in a completely illegitimate way. These moments are not uncommon for many of us but there are people who are precisely to divinely put in your life just to be your friend and not your lover!

Characteristic of a Good Friend.

➤ A friend should "never" be chosen instantly! Real friends grow into your life... they start with few things and if in time they are trustworthy and true, they end up entrusted with many levels of your life and the title good friend!

➤ Friends carry their own weight in the friendship... no vantage taking! Both bring value and benefit to the relationship albeit what they each bring is different!

➤ Friends sometimes disagree and need space. They keep each other at the right distance. Friends don't always feel or think the same but its ok if they're not together every moment during those transitions. Friends allow friends to grow and evolve like they should, and when a friend is in transition the other supports and encourages that. There is beauty and a blessing in supporting a friend through real life transitions.

➢ Just because you talked to someone about your life and problems, doesn't mean that they are "Friend" material! True "friend material" comes with understanding, acceptance, motivation, and direction, to offer. You can talk to a stranger, psychiatrist, or a dog… it doesn't make them a friend!

➢ A friend comes with two unique qualities… They can both, learn from you and teach you something! Friends have mercy on each other but they don't give passes when you're wrong, if you're wrong, you're wrong! A friend is always on the side of "Fair"

➢ Friendship is proven and tested through consistency, trustworthiness, and wisdom. Friends demonstrate these characteristics towards one another when a friend is experiencing a season of growth or change in their life!

These are just some of the fundamental characteristics you can look for in order to discern people who truly fit, and should be regarded as a friend.

Sex ReWorked

I Just Want To See You Strip

It is my prayer that as you read the words of this chapter you will start to strip and get undressed. Try and relax while you uncover your private parts and release the biggest spiritual orgasmic sigh of relief you've ever had. Learn yourself as you take off your shame and your guilt about your sexuality. Your sexuality is your sexual personality. Some people are aggressive and some people are passive, some like a lot and for others, a little dab will do. It is who you are sexually, you are not just spiritual or just natural you are very sexual. The goal is for you to be able to experience and express your sexuality. Denying it will only make you deficient, disturbed, and destructive. The topic of sex and sexuality are one of the most mysterious and misunderstood subjects of the human experience. There aren't many resources available that offer real guidance on the subject of sex! How should we think about it, how to responsibly maintain it, experience it, and benefit from it! My question and many other's questions are, who is to provide guidance about sex?

The medical field advocates for safe sex and encourages abstinence as the safest way. But there purpose is medicine and treating the causes and symptoms of sickness, not giving guidance on human sexuality. The public school system offers sex education, it defines the sex organs and how they function, but no guidance on the, what, when, and how of human sexuality. Parents are shaking in their boots because they are ashamed, insecure, and heartbroken because they can't save their children anymore than they could save themselves. But the church, since sex is created by God, and is centrally tied to our physical existence, you would think the church would have something meaningful to say about sex. The Catholic Church can't come to terms with their own self-condemning doctrine on sexuality. They can't see how to reconcile it with the widespread sexual sins of their priesthood for the last 100 years or more. The protestant church or mainstream Christian church has spent the last 700 years passionately dressing human sexuality in guilt and shame making it sinful, nasty, and a taboo subject. Which only made sex more prurient and exaggerated than it would normally be.

Why is there no real, meaningful guidance about sex? The reason is religion is arrogant, narcissistic, and puffed up, which is a nice way of saying it is idolatrous! Religion is bent on acting like it has every answer even when it has no answers! Religion will never ever admit that it was wrong about anything ever! It doesn't have the capacity to do so! The Christian and Catholic Church are inundated with sexual dysfunction and sin, not because people are rank and bad, or that a devil or evil is that strong! The church is ravaged because of a lack of direction and understanding about sex! "Don't Do it" and "Wait till your married" are not instructions and directions that bring any understanding to a person's sexuality. So if the ones who say they represent God (the church) are struggling and suffering without an answer, what hope does the world sitting on the peripheral have?

Extreme behaviors such as incest, pedophilia, and adultery, I believe find some of there cause in the suppression and the repression of human sexuality mainly from religion. People simply reject and suppress what they don't understand.

There's a Jewish proverb that says, "In all thy getting, get an understanding" There are two different kinds of understanding that you need in order to have a healthy concept of anything. There is the simple understanding and the central understanding. The simple understanding of a thing is the obvious, surface, shallow understanding of the concept. These simple understanding is often passed down with irrelevant meanings to modern society and handed to us as the full concept. The central understanding of a thing is the essence and fundamental meaning it carries first of all. If you wanted to understand strength you don't study force, you study resilience. Strength is the ability to recuperate, recover, and remain! If you wanted to understand marriage you don't study faithfulness, you study covenant! Marriage is about a person agreeing to terms then fulfilling and being faithful to what they committed to do regardless of what the other is doing! Likewise if you want to understand sex you don't study pornography, you study human nature or human sexuality! Our simple understanding of sex is that it must be done in the confines of marriage or it is perceived to be nasty, perverted, and damning!

The central understanding of sex is it is innate and divinely inspired by God. It was created for pleasure and procreation! God creates it in all, for all without mankind's consent! It is a part or our physiological make up. You need both the central and simple understanding of sexuality in order to accurately and fully understand sex or your sexuality. Along with what was passed down to us we have to add science, wisdom, and culture to it if we want to be complete and accurate. Just saying, "wait until you get married to even think about sex" would be great if your sexuality was an update that you downloaded after you said I do, but the truth is you were born with your sexuality. It is a God given and divine endowment by God, and it's about time we say it! Your sexuality is a part of your physiology and you don't have to do anything salacious to become turned on, horny or to have a wet dream (orgasm)! It is critical for you to take off and rid yourself of the shame and guilt that has been attached to your sexuality! There is a Godly and healthy way for you to experience and to express it. I just wanna see you strip!

Sex and the Bible

When we look at the bible we find that sexual energy is present at the very beginning of the documents of scripture and encouraged by God. At the onset and first mention of the world, mankind, and life in scripture it says, "God blessed them," and then God commanded the man and woman to, "Be fruitful and multiply!" Genesis 1:28 First God blessed the man and woman. To bless is to, bestow, impart, and to favor. The question is what did God bless them with? God blessed them with validation and affirmation, His love! God in that moment sanctioned the man and woman to embrace every state, condition, and quality He had created in them and for them! Their, humanity, mentality, personality, spirituality and yes their sexuality! Your sexuality is a part of the blessing of the Lord! Then God says to them, "Be fruitful and multiply" to be fruitful means to be productive, creative, constructive, or fertile. To multiply means to bear, procreate, generate, mate, or breed! These commandments by God in scripture clearly suggest and promote reproduction.

Weather you're speaking of the reproduction of plants, animals, ideas, or human beings, sexual energy is always present and the primal cause of the reproduction of all living things. Anything that is living and has been brought forth or begat through reproduction was spawned by sexual energy. We find God 12 chapters later at what is arguably the next most significant milestone in the life of Christianity in Genesis 12:1-12. Where God blesses Abram and His Seed. The bible reveals Abrams seed as Christ. God says; in thee and thy seed shall all of the families of the earth be blessed. Here God is speaking about generational blessings, but you can't have a generation without generating or procreating first! The point is God referencing Abram's "seed" which is located in his loins or sexual reproductive organs suggest again that sex is the blessed medium and method through which men and women will fulfill that blessed commandment to be fruitful and multiply. It is hard to believe that the means that God uses to sponsor all living things including all of mankind could be the object of such ridicule and negativity.

All throughout the documents of scripture you will find constant references directly or indirectly to human sexuality, sex, seeds, conception, pregnancy, birth, reproduction, physical pleasure, masturbation, rape, adultery, fornication, prostitution, adolescence, babies, bestiality, homosexuality, kissing, incest, bareness, miscarriages, wombs, eunuchs, semen, and sodomy! When the church finds this many scriptures that speak directly or indirectly in types and shadows on any other subject they have a movement or at least an established doctrine on the subject. They find scriptures on the Holy Spirit, so they have a Holy Ghost Revival, they find hundreds of scriptures on money most of which are indirect mentions about money but they don't just have a revival, they have a whole movement called prosperity teaching! But look at all the scriptures about sex and the thousands of references to it and the only thing the church has to say is... Don't do it until you get married!

I am convinced that neither God, nor the bible has a problem with sex, but religious people do!

Religious people assume that God endorses marriage with the, "two shall become one flesh" scripture, but is that an endorsement or even a reference to marriage as we know it? In scripture we find the idea of two becoming one flesh, this was simply when a man and a woman cut covenant with one another and consummated that covenant or agreement by engaging in sexual intercourse. The idea of becoming one flesh does not carry with it any innate vows, specifics, or commands. It is sexual consent autonomously agreed upon between the man and the woman to engage in sex! The exchange for sex is not marriage the exchange for sex is sex! Becoming one flesh with someone represents one of the highest forms of connection. However, the introduction of marriage as a sacrament of the Church constrained the idea of "two becoming one flesh" to belong only within the confines of marriage in a very sinister way. This change in the idea of basic connection caused sex and sexuality to become the scapegoat and villain in the narrative of two becoming one flesh.

One of the more famous and scandalous scriptures involving sex portrays this idea. Jesus meets a woman at a well who was there to draw water to drink. In this narrative Jesus makes the statement that the woman has 7 husbands and the one she was currently with was not hers'! In Jewish thought when a woman cut covenant and rendered sex to a man she was regarded as his wife or one flesh with him. The thrust of this age-old idea was "property," the woman was a possession of her father or the man. This statement by Jesus demonstrates the ideals of the culture in biblical times not some new Christian doctrine we made up. This scripture was not making a case that sex outside of marriage causes you to be connected to another person in an ungodly way. It was not about whether this woman was a prostitute or not. It was not about if she was a promiscuous woman entertaining various different men. It wasn't about her falling in love at all, and it was not an endorsement of marriage as God's best for everybody!

People attempt to make this story about sex, marriage, or a woman deeply caught up in sin and sexual misconduct but this story has nothing to do with the woman's sex life or any of her sins. Jesus' intent in the text was to communicate that we as human beings will experience certain voids that can only be fully filled and satisfied by the presence of God and Spiritual consciousness! Two becoming one flesh outside the confines of marriage has become an ominous scare tactic to prohibit premarital sex among the masses. While I am not advocating for premarital sex, this distortion of the concept is misleading and not profitable. Perpetuating the lie that everybody you have a sexual encounter with who isn't your husband or wife is somehow negatively affecting you or is perverting your spirit somehow is disingenuous. It's about time that we just say it; men have hijacked the bible with their own fear filled interpretations of scripture and have bought into those fears; mind, body, and soul. Sex is not God's focus or His enemy in scripture or with relationship period. Connection on any level should be regarded as one of the purest of all human processes.

A lot of the misconception concerning sex and whether it is legal or not, is a result of a bad definition for the act of fornication. We will deal with the correct definition of fornication at length in a later chapter. Denying yourself the ability to acknowledge your sexuality may seem noble and strong in spirit, but don't sign God's signature to that position. Don't think or infer that by sacrificing your sexual sense of self that you are in God's perfect will or that this honors Him. God would much rather you deny hate, being judgmental, and being fearful far more than you denying your human sexuality! As you'll see in other chapters, sex has to do with physiology and sensuality. Many people of faith view sex to be a great evil. The idea that God created human sexuality and at the same time Him viewing it as evil is ridiculous! There is no scripture to support this as God's position! The belief that God wants to punish those who act out of their sexuality is misleading and a distortion of the truth. The truth about sex is self evident, in life, in application, and in scripture. This truth requires us to reconsider what we hold to as right.

These truths are self-evident and they compel us to reconsider our interpretation of the scriptures. Most of the practices passed on to us have not been scrutinized through the light of God as it pertains to today's culture and people! Sex and faith are so deeply entwined in the ideas of most people that we have to note the sway and influence religion has on love, sex and marriage in modern society. Men and women, particularly of the Christian faith, have a bad tendency to stretch the scriptures out of context in order to bring about their own will, rather than giving rise to the will of God. These people use the scriptures to justify whatever they deem permissible, and equally use the scriptures to reject and condemn anything they deem not good or worthy. One example of stretching scripture out of context to fit personal preference is when we contrast women in ministry roles in the bible verses sex in the bible. The bible speaks emphatically about women in leadership roles over men but says nothing remotely emphatic about sex being evil. Yet, they find a way around the deliberate statements about women in authority then they make up an interpretation to suppress human sexuality.

For example in I Timothy 2:11-13 the scripture emphatically says, 11A woman must quietly receive instruction with entire submissiveness. 12But I do not allow a woman to teach or exercise authority over a man, but to remain quiet. 13For it was Adam who was first created, and then Eve. This is not ambiguous at all. A woman according to scripture should be quiet and submit to the authority of a man and must not take authority over them! This is not unclear, however, when it comes to sex in the bible there is no emphatic declarative statement that sex is innately wrong or sinful. These same people who overlook the exact prohibition of women ruling or teaching men, take scriptures like 1 Corinthians 7:1-9 and stretch it out of context in order to bring about what they believe is right. These scriptures were speaking to people about not stealing another man's property. These texts were about not violating your brothers in the community. It was also about not being given to idol worship or any sexual sin that may result in defilement before God, which was prevalent in the city of Corinth at the time these texts were being written. It is a stretch to interpret them to be about marriage or the sanctity of the institution itself.

As we can clearly see, Paul goes on late in verses 6 and 7 to say, I speak these scriptures as "concessions" and not as "commandments!" Then Paul goes further and says, "Keep in mind we all have different gifts and abilities given by God. Paul is clearly saying that these are not God's commands! So why would we turn around and create some law out of these scriptures and then teach them as commands? Paul also says, what one can handle is different than what another can handle! This is just an example of how people can take a line of scriptures and use them to advance personal agendas rather than God's agenda. For example, it would be foolish for me to take first Corinthians chapter seven, in verse one where Paul says; "it is good for a man "not" to touch a woman." If I then stretch this verse out of context to be an endorsement of homosexuality, and say men should lay with men that would be taking the verse out of context. Though based on a literal interpretation of this single verse I could say it was inferred. Can you see how ridiculous it is to take a few verses out of their full context in an attempt to advance a personal agenda?

All throughout the bible when you see sexual indiscretion, many times it ends up finding the woman at fault. With Sarah and Abraham, Sarah ends up looking like the only one who doubted God and went around God's plan to give her and Abraham the promised son, when in fact Sarah and Abraham both agreed to engage with her handmaiden Hagar. So she gave him Hagar in order to have the promised son after she couldn't get pregnant. This doesn't speak to doubt as much as it speaks to the reality of their circumstances. Then, we have Lot's daughters who are cast in a negative light when they seem to be wayward girls violating there own father by getting him drunk with wine and having sexual intercourse with him. When the context says, they had run out of Sodom and watched God destroy the men of the city and along with their mother who was turned into a pillar of salt. Their belief was that they were the only women left and all of the men had perished also, so by instinct and cultural conditioning they decided to have offspring even if that meant having sex with their own father. During this time-period it was that serious for a woman to have children.

By doing this they did defile their father but culture, their past experiences, along with the pressure to survive and have a since of honor cannot be absolved of blame for their actions. Then there is the woman caught in adultery; the scripture says in the very act of it. It is curious that a woman is dragged out of the shadows to be ridiculed and judged, but no male is treated in this way. This woman had her shortcoming put on spotlight and she fell in danger of being stoned to death! We don't know if this woman's adultery had anything to do with another person or some form of idol worship, the scripture does not tell us what it was. This passage was not about adultery or guilt of any kind, the passage was really about forgiveness. The truth and thrust of this narrative was that we all stand guilty of something before the eyes of God but forgiveness is available and is morally correct and honorable. For the record it is no secret that women are done a dis-service in biblical culture when it comes to sexuality. And men were usually never held responsible for their transgressions and trespasses because, of course, the men were the ones making up and enforcing all the rules!

When we look at the explicit sexual nature of the Song of Solomon, also known as the Song of Songs, these texts have puzzled biblical scholars for centuries. Scholars have wondered how could such an erotic text be considered and accepted as Holy Scripture. The hyper-sensuality of the text is literally a contradiction to the interpretations of modern Christians and their emphatic suppression of human sexuality. Theologians and Rabbis came along and over time, changed the essence of this sexual hymn written by Solomon into an allegory of the love between God and Ancient Israel. Then, mainstream Christians came centuries later and changed it into an allegory of the love Christ has for the Church. All of this is an attempt to qualify and position such an erotic text as just spiritual metaphor to teach the truth of God's love! When in fact this is a super sexual account of passion and raw sex between Solomon and a women he possessed a deeply intimate connection with. These scriptures are plain and simply about sex! You can't frame it in marriage and rob it of its erotica or its demonstration of the passion of human sexuality!

You can't say because they were married it makes the sex honorable, because Solomon and this woman were not married like we are, their model of marriage was not the model we use today! Beyond appreciating Solomon's hymn as a piece of powerful literature that teaches us the depths of human sexuality in the presence of God. For anyone to go any further in interpreting this text otherwise is to precisely distort the truth! This doesn't mean the story of King Solomon isn't divinely inspired, it simply means that the story doesn't support our misinterpretations of scripture, our declaration that sex and traditional marriage are inextricably tied together, or our paranoia about premarital sex leading to curses or perversion. It is better to accept the Song of Solomon exactly for what it is, a sexually explicit and sensual account of some of the raciest physical sex engaged in by a man and woman! It was an account of what he did, what she did, and how it made them feel and physically react! Rather than sex being at odds with God and the scriptures, sex just may be the most intense expression of spirituality that glorifies and sanctifies the passion from which all life is spawn.

Pre-Marital Sex & Fornication

Fornication is commonly known as any sexual activity outside of the covenant of marriage or to put it another way pre-marital sex. Fornication or pre-marital sex in the eyes of a lot of Christians is the supreme and worst sin that could be committed. It seems that it would be better if you told a lie, took drugs, or stole money rather than to have sex before you got married. It's as if fornication is worse than all the other sins or more derogatory or filthy in some way. The shocking truth about fornication is many people actually engage in pre-marital sex but deeply believe that they are sinning against God and offending Him. Everyone from pastors, judges, lawyers, teachers, bus drivers, tv and movie stars, young people, seniors, politicians, police, psychologist and presidents all have sex before marriage. Literally people from all walks of life engage in some form of pre-marital sex and they wrestle with the burden of guilt asking God to forgive them afterwards. Then they go through a mental ritual to rid themselves of the shame that ensues after having sex, only to do it all over again.

The bible talks a great deal about the sin of fornication and sexual immorality. For the record fornication is sin and so is sexual immorality, neither of which have anything at all to do with premarital sex! The problem we have today is ordinary flawed men were given an absurd amount of influence over fashioning the Christian faith through their fear, interpretations and legalism. These men were given a massive amount of authority from other men to dictate the spirituality of hundreds of generations of believers without challenge! What I am doing is bringing to light the proof of the truth that exist even though mainstream Christianity doesn't want you to know it! Frankly I'm amazed that there aren't more Christian teachers, doctors, and preachers seeking to correct this error. You should not pay attention to Christians who keep throwing out the same broken declaration that sex was created by God to feel good and be amazing but only in the confines of marriage! Shut up already! These people are not helping anybody, the single, the married, the desperate, or the dysfunctional!

You can't know the truth about what God says is sexually right or wrong by reading six or seven verses from the bible with some bias teacher in your ear telling you what it all means and redefining the words to say how bad sex is! You can't know the truth by allowing the Christian majority to push you into error without challenging it! Did your mother ever tell you to think for yourself and don't be a follower, this would be the perfect time to obey your mother!

How we got tangled up and confused about consenting adults having sex, sin, and marriage, is a long story but let me make a long story short! Sexual immorality and fornication from Genesis to Revelations has **always meant** "temple prostitution," sexual acts in worship of other Gods, incest, pedophilia, rape, orgies, and adultery! Because of culture, lack of understanding, mistranslations, and assumptions, men have "literally" changed the definition of fornication to mean, **SEX BEFORE MARRIAGE!!!!** But, the bible has never said such a thing!

The only way the bible says sex before marriage is sin in God's eyes, is if you change the definition of fornication from prostitution and idolatry to mean, **"any sex before marriage"**! In so many books men have written about God, sex and the bible you will find this flawed definition of sex. You will find it everywhere except for, in the bible. And just because it's written wrong a lot of times by a lot of people still does not make it right! You won't find the definition we have in modern culture for fornication anywhere in the bible! Where exactly did everything right go left! The meaning of the word fornication got lost in transliteration by motivation! By transliteration I mean religious men translated the scripture from its original language into another language using the "closest letters and words" to fit the secondary language. By motivation I mean that which prompted their particular reasoning. Their motivation was; fear, manipulation, and absolute control mixed with self-righteousness. Basically religious men took the word fornication and began to define it based on their own fears and superstitions.

These flawed perspectives were likely influenced by other broken and controlling men from various other cultures and religions. When truth gets lost, "truth tellers" will attempt to re-establish the truth, but the men in error with unchecked pride tend to respond with rejection, suppression, and rage! Even when being faced with irrefutable facts.

No matter what century or what the circumstances are, all believers have a responsibility to seek God's voice and receive revelation knowledge from Him, the kind of revelation that flesh and blood does not reveal! Watch Jesus' perspective, every time Jesus mentions fornication in the bible He is literally talking about marriages facing divorce because someone in the marriage has committed fornication. If Jesus defined fornication as we do in modern culture today, how can you commit fornication if you're married?

Darrell L. Owens

In the 1600's when King James sanctioned and ordered the Hebrew Old testament and the Greek New Testament scriptures translated into the king's English, this brought us the "King James Bible" this was the point in history where Greek and English speaking scholars of that day chose and used the English word fornication as the English translation of the Latin word Fornix or Fonicare and the Greek word porniea. The word Fornication itself is an English word. It is not Greek, it is not Latin, and it is not Hebrew. It was introduced in the 1300's but before the 1300's the word either did not exist or had never been used. When the word fornication was introduced to the English language it's meaning was the same as the Greek and Latin words it was derived from. "Fornication" was the English way of saying both the Greek word porniea and the Latin word Fornix or Fonicare. These three words all meant the same thing temple prostitution, idolatry, incest, rape, pedophilia, orgies and adultery. The writers of the bible while being inspired wrote the scriptures in their own ancient language and definition.

Before the word fornication was spoken or written the ancients actually used the Hebrew word Zanah and the Greek word Porniea to identify and condemn all illicit acts of sex unto idols or illegal acts of sex towards kinsmen! Today most modern translations of the bible don't use fornication any more they use "sexual immorality." So the 26 times you find the word fornication or sexual immorality in the New Testament you may read, sexual immorality or fornication just remember the actual word that was originally written was porniea not fornication or sexual immorality. Remember porniea has a meaning and it's not "sex before marriage"! The confusion really begins with early church fathers, their theology, their interpretations, their limited vantage points, and the pagan religions they were influenced by. This is what really sent the spirituality and sexuality of several generations of Christians over a cliff!

The church fathers, men such as: the Apostle Paul, Tertullian, St. Jerome, Augustine of Hippo (Algeria) they all had enormous influence over what modern Christians believe or accept as fundamental truth and righteousness, even today! They lost and or changed the definition of fornication by interpreting it's meaning to be no sex before marriage! They laid out doctrines that were based off of and sponsored by the culture and the pagan religions that existed around them! They were pre-disposed emotionally with certain biases that colored their experiences and shaped their beliefs. You won't find them using love as their guide for the decisions and the drama they created amongst seekers of God even though this is the light that Jesus left some 300 years earlier! These men were basically anti-sex, anti- woman, and anti- social! Yes, they used their religion to justify sexism against women, racism against other races, and the condemnation of sexuality in general!! These men misunderstood and mistook culture and history for the will of God, and this was a grave misstep!

The church fathers and teachers in the Common Era some 250 to

300 years after the life of Jesus were Christian ascetics. Meaning

they were extreme and strict in their beliefs about the material

world and believed that only spiritual things had worth, or value.

They were against any expression of sex or human sexuality.

These church fathers would set the course of sexual ethics for the

Catholic and Christian church for the next 18 centuries! Their

extremism, convictions, and perspectives perpetuated disrespect

for women, human sexuality, and for truth itself. These culturally

based church leaders believed that salvation and spirituality

could be attained through strict adherence to religious law,

sexual abstinence, and severe self-denial. These convictions

were obviously cultural and man-made and rooted in other pagan

religions in the region. These men lived more than a century

after the first gospel was written about Jesus. It is very

conceivable that their interpretation of what Jesus said and meant

was distorted, and a great distance away from the truth he taught

and lived! These archaic and dysfunctional beliefs reach as far as

the 20th century, affecting us still today!

The church father and theologian named Tertullian was regarded as the father of American theology. He was known as a strict polemicist, one who upholds order like a Sargent of Arms. He was an apologist, one who felt appointed to defend the faith or God's will as it was revealed to him! St. Jerome was another church father who, is known mostly for translating the original Greek scriptures into Latin. Which today is known as the Latin Vulgate bible. He was also very popular for interpreting and outlining proper Christian ethics and behavior for Christians collectively! Then there was Augustine of Algeria, who was one of the most influential fathers of American Christian doctrine. All of these men helped shape the Christian view of woman, sexuality, and righteousness! These among other church fathers were so extreme at points they taught and forbid men to have sex with their own wives calling sex even in marriage fornication. Some believed that women today still carry the judgment of God on them and referred to women in general as "Eve"! They would women are the Devil's gateway.

They believed women literally unsealed the curse of the tree and believed that women were the ones who persuaded the man whom the devil could not corrupt, and she was worthy of death! They said things like, corruption was attached to all intercourse, and incorruption was a sign of chastity or the rewards of chastity could not belong to two in marriage! These were actually beliefs of the Christian fathers who carried enormous influence on the beliefs and interpretation of sex and the sexual ethics of Christendom many years after the death of Jesus. It would be at the top of the 20st Century before the Protestant or Christian church would ultimately break away from these stringent beliefs and reject the idea that even, "sex within a marriage" was spiritually harmful. It wouldn't be until the middle of the 21st century that women would find freedom from these extreme men, and be granted the ability to preach, teach, and generally be respected! Fortunately as time would pass these misguided interpretations would slowly begin to be watered down, changed, adjusted, rejected, and some finally completely done away with.

However the erroneous doctrine that re-defined the sin of fornication as "sex before marriage" has survived the test of time! Some may accuse me of trying to change the definition of fornication, well yes I want to change it back to what it has always meant since forever! Let's look back, for a point of reference, it was the spiritual and sexual dysfunction of Hebrew culture in the Old Testament that spawned the Hebrew Scriptures that even reference illegal sex, immorality or idol worship! It was never sex between two consenting autonomous adults having sex or expressing themselves sexually that produced the scriptures we read in the Old and New Testaments! In the Old Testament the word was 'Zanah' which was translated into the Greek word 'Porniea' which was translated into the English word 'Fornication'. These three words mean the same thing. Sexual Immorality would be the modern and umbrella term that would incorporate all the specific sins that the bible refers to when it uses the term fornication. Fornication consisted of; chiefly temple prostitution, idolatry, incest, rape, pedophilia, orgies and adultery it also included consuming foods offered to idols!

All of these practices were illegal and possessed some idolatrous aspect to them in scripture! In biblical times the cords of sexuality and spirituality were considerably crossed. People often had divided loyalties between Jehovah God and other pagan deities. People used sex as a form and way of worshiping and giving sacrifices unto idol gods. So, God enacted covenants and laws in order to repent his people back from their idolatry and to stop the offense His own people had become to Him. The key thing to remember is, God accused His people "collectively" of fornication and harlotry or husbands and wives of adultery. It was never God watching individuals engaged in consensual pre-marital sex and charging them with the sin of "fornication"! The sin of fornication was about the acts and positions of the heart that compromised covenant between God and His people or husbands and their wives! This is the Old Testament backdrop for where Jesus would introduce grace to the world.

The idea that God would create human beings biologically with a sexuality, give us a desire for sex, then command us to resist that desire for sex to prove our love for Him would be deranged and confusing. Our clergy today talk with great concern about sex being sinful, but they can't stop agonizing and lusting for it themselves! The bible is full of allegories, which are metaphors, parables, and analogies. It uses phrases and words as symbols to refer to deeper meanings and spiritual truth.

In order to know the meaning of scripture and to know its truth you have to measure all scripture beside love. Then respect context and hold reverence for the facts, these all serve as filters for what the scriptures reveal. No where in the bible will you find a single scripture that says, explicitly or metaphorically that "pre-marital sex" is a sin! Unless of course you still believe that pre-marital sex is fornication, which it is not! Hear are a few of the main scriptures people use to infer that pre-marital sex is the same as fornication and sexual immorality.

Genesis 2:24 "Therefore a man shall leave his father and his mother and be joined to his wife, and they shall become one flesh."

With this verse people assume, God wants you to remain at the status you were with your parents until you get married. Most don't realize that men and women married at a very young age in biblical culture and this is what makes traditional culture think that marriage is obviously the right or the God way to go. To some this verse implies that any kind of sex before marriage is sin, they assume the scripture is saying a man should leave his parents house and go straight way into marriage with a woman. They interpret this to mean, this was the only woman he was to have sex with.

Rework: As you can plainly read the scripture doesn't explicitly say sex before marriage is sin and it hardly implies it. While the idea of becoming one flesh "begins" with sexual consummation, becoming one flesh has more to do with agreement, unity, and love. The first thing that you should take note of is the context of the scripture.

This scripture was not a declaration of the will of God, that everybody is to get married. It was not a prohibition of sex before marriage that you can't have sex until you've found a wife or a husband! Verse 24 was the effect for which verse 23 was the cause. Verse 23 says, the man said, "This is now bone of my bones and flesh of my flesh; she shall be called "woman" for she was taken out of man. Verse 24 says, "therefore" meaning, because of verse 23, or this is why, a man shall leave his father and mother and be joined to his wife! The first obvious truth is that men were made for women and women for men! Secondly it presents the opportunity to experience wholeness through companionship or being one in spirit with another. Thirdly it is the reconnection of the man and the woman, who by creation were originally one. Marriage represents them returning back to their point of origin or essential essence. There is nothing about pre-marital sex being sinful in this scripture or the same as fornication!

1 Corinthians 6:13 "Food is meant for the stomach and the stomach for food —and God will destroy both one and the other. The body is not meant for sexual immorality, but for the Lord, and the Lord for the body."

The assumption about this verse is that sexual immorality or the word porniea mean any sex outside of marriage. Or the assumption that people should keep themselves from any sex before marriage and that we should give ourselves totally to God, that's what our bodies were made for!

Rework: If you change the definition of sexual immorality, which is porniea to mean pre-marital sex, maybe you'd be right. But if you tell the truth, the terms sexual immorality and porniea mean idolatry, illicit sex, and prostitution. Only then will the scripture be accurate and honest! Now read it again honestly and the scripture will say, food and the stomach go together but both will pass away. The food will digest and be eliminated and the stomach will decompose when the person has physically died.

The reference to food and the stomach is a direct reference to the overwhelming amount of scriptures warning ancient culture against eating foods sacrificed to idols! The reference to sexual immorality was a direct prohibition of sex as an act offered in worship to idols. The body is not meant for prostitution, pedophilia, incest, and the worship of idol gods! The body being meant for the lord was a metaphor for spiritually worshiping another god beside the true God! This is the context in which St. Paul is writing this verse. There is nothing about pre-marital sex being sinful in this scripture or the same as fornication!

1 Corinthians 7:1-4 "Now concerning the things wherefore ye wrote unto me: It is good for a man not to touch a woman. Nevertheless, to avoid fornication, let every man have his own wife, and let every woman have her own husband. Let the husband render unto the wife due benevolence: and likewise also the wife unto the husband."

The assumptive interpretation of this verse is the only way to avoid falling into fornication is to have a wife or a husband!

The notion that being married will keep you free from the sin of fornication is outright wrong!

Rework: Tell the truth! If fornication did mean sex before marriage, the people listening to Paul wouldn't be able to fornicate because they were already married! Right? Paul says, "have your own wife and husband" On the other hand this couldn't mean you need to get married to avoid fornication because then why would Jesus in Matthew 5:32 say, "whoever divorces his wife for any reason except sexual immorality (which is porniea which means the same thing as fornication) causes her to commit adultery?" We see then, defining fornication as premarital sex is extremely wrong! How can you fornicate when your already married? If fornication means pre-marital sex? You got to tell the truth! There is nothing about pre-marital sex being sinful in this scripture or the same as fornication!

Hebrews 13:4 "Let marriage be held in honor among all, and let the marriage bed be undefiled, for God will judge the sexually immoral and adulterous."

The assumption here is that marriage as we believe it and teach it is God's way or His idea! As if God is judging people who don't respect the concept of traditional marriage. Like God Himself instituted what we practice today. This is a grave misconception! They assume this means married couples can get as nasty and freaky as they would like to, but you "pre-marital sexers," hear this!!! When the bible says, "the sexually immoral" it means all of you having sex outside of marriage, and God will judge you and send you to hell.

Rework: The scripture literally says, "let the marriage bed be undefiled" then it goes on and says in conjunction "for God will judge the sexually immoral and the adulterous." These two statements go together. The marriage bed would be defiled by "actual" sexual immorality. Which would be two people married but practicing some form of idolatry or sexual worship.

Possibly participating in a form of prostitution or sexual deviance as an act of worship, not pre-marital sex! Those who were married needed to honor their marriage and their sexuality by not participating in any idol worship. This is what defiled these marriages and the individuals. There is nothing about pre-marital sex being sinful in this scripture or anything that identifies premarital sex as being the same thing as fornication! I can see how these verses could get twisted if all you wanted to do is prove a misguided point taught by man. I can see how it gets confusing if all you want to do is reinforce fear and make people comfortable in their ignorance. But if you care about the truth based on the facts. You will have to deny your comfort and betray pride to have the truth! The definition of words and symbols can't just be whatever you want them to be. You can't just accept a definition as truth because a lot of people have agreed to a wrong definition. You have to be objective. You have to tell the truth even if it doesn't support what you believe, or what feels right to you. We know now that fornication by definition is the prohibition of any unlawful or unsanctioned sexual activity.

We know that pre-marital sex is any sex before getting married. What needs to be made clear is that these two are not one and the same. We cannot live based off of the wrong beliefs shared in this chapter. You should not ignore your sexuality nor the spirit of God. I don't intend on standing by and watching people live under pressure and in bondage. Not the pressure of needing to have sex, or the bondage of the prohibition of sex. I'm talking about the pressure that come from guilt and the shame about being sexual and having a sexuality. Whether you're married or not you must honor your sexuality and meet your sexual needs in legitimate ways. It is my prayer that you escape the dysfunctional notion that ignoring your sexuality will produce Godliness. These beliefs about pre-marital sex have made many people feel unworthy of God and His love. This has been a distraction for all of us from living fully and exceptionally. This is not an endorsement to be sexually reckless, it is your opportunity to resist lies and the confusion men produce and begin to live abundantly.

Masturbation

The subject of masturbation has always been somewhat taboo and untouched in modern society! This is because religion has spent much of the last 250 years trying to make people righteous and somehow holy by demonizing human sexuality. Introducing shame and guilt as the tools by which it does this. This, on a deeper level has also been about religion's need and attempt to control others, not realizing that these strategies may work to manipulate the mind but have no affect on the heart. The obvious question most people have about masturbation is, is it permissible or is it a sin? I hope to answer that for you now. If you talk about masturbation purely in the context of religious right or wrong you start from a distorted point of view because masturbation is all about human sexuality and has very little to do with morality, the will of God, or right and wrong because we have already established that our sexuality is divinely given to us by God the creator.

Think about the fundamental definition of masturbation; the physical pleasuring of one's self. Masturbation is physical, it is self-motivated, and is mainly experienced by self. How have we turned this into a sin and some immoral act before God? Ask any respected theologian if the bible anywhere addresses the subject of masturbation and they will tell you no! Later on we will explore some the documents of scripture that people stretch out of context trying to make it illegal to masturbate. The truth is the medical and psychiatric community have established and attributed many benefits for a person with a healthy attitude towards their sexuality in general and towards masturbation in particular. Doctors now know because of the people that they treat, and the generations of study that have shown them, if a person has an unhealthy relationship towards their sexuality there is a direct tie between them becoming self destructive and dangerous to the community in which they live! I have a devout very faithful friend name Stoney who really loves God and walks the walk. She lives the life that she believes God would have her to live.

However Stoney said to me one day regarding this subject that masturbation was "self worship and un-natural" my response was; worship adds value to something and nobody uses masturbation to add value to themselves or to establish their own worth. So it can't be self-worship. Then it couldn't be un-natural because we know that pleasure, sexual arousal, and physical satisfaction are very natural, personal and amoral! We also know that the physical process we call, "getting turned on" or sexually aroused is all a physical and biological process that needs no external stimuli to occur. Doctors will tell you that even babies operate in some form of self- pleasuring from day one. Weather its finding comfort laying on the breast of the mother or gently humping the bed on their stomach. Both are a forms of seeking to please or pleasure one's self even if the goal is not to obtain an orgasm! So on one hand I really do get Stoney's conviction and belief system, but on the other hand I don't get why we don't want to acknowledge these plain facts that are self evident without introducing interpretations and personal persuasions concerning; God, sex, and the bible!

Some of the wrong beliefs about masturbation range from; it would make you sterile, desensitize you, give you acne, all the way to the belief that it would make you blind or create some form of insanity. These kinds of absurd notions are rooted in religious arrogance and hysteria! Religion makes the case that it is a slippery slope and that it would spiral one into deep sexual perversion. A person carrying guilt and shame about their sexuality is far more disturbed than a person who regularly masturbates. This too is self-evident and based on multiple studies! In a study from Duke University researchers found after following 252 people over 25 years concluded that there was a clear correlation between a healthy sex life (having multiple orgasms 2 or 3 a week) and looking and feeling up to six years younger. The idea that masturbation is a slippery slope to sexual dysfunction and perversion is unfounded. The idea that pleasuring yourself leads you into any kind of dysfunction is foolish and without merit. I don't need statistics to prove this it is a self-evident truth.

Take an anonymous poll in your group, church, or class and see how many people will say it was masturbation that perverted them and see the results your self! Frankly, the opposite is true about perversion. It is the guilt ridden and the person who is filled with shame that struggles the most with perversion and unhealthy practices. When people feel ashamed and uninformed about their sexuality and the sexual urges they cannot deny, they tend to spiral out of control and into sexual fantasy void of truth and freedom. This creates a sense of desperation within the soul, which fosters a very dark state of mind that can lead to behaviors like rape, molestation, and obsessive and compulsive people that prey on the innocent of society! It is my firm belief that the whole truth of the fall out in the Catholic Church hasn't been told! The money and power the Catholic Church possesses has definitely softened the blow and masked more grave crimes than they will ever admit to!

But just looking at the overwhelming amount of instances that have been exposed against thousands of young boys coast to coast and abroad, this wasn't just a small indiscretion by a hand full of priest it was most certainly systemic and a part of the culture of the priesthood in general not being allowed to experience, express, or explore their own sexuality! Masturbation would be a great adjustment for priest if they choose to remain single and non-sexual with another. The decision not to engage in sexual activity and to remain holy and only unto the Lord can be reworked and done differently.

The point is that masturbation is not a spiritual or a moral issue beyond the stigma placed on anyone engaging in the act of masturbation. There is no place in scripture where masturbation is even mentioned, much less forbidden. Its about time we said that and moved on from that pious and ridiculous stance against masturbation! Let's look at the one main verse in scripture many people try to stretch to mean masturbation is sinful and unnatural!

In Genesis 38:1-11 you find the story of a man named Judah with three sons and a daughter in law named Tamar. Tamar was married to Judah's oldest son Er. Er was wicked and God killed him, and as it was their custom the brother in law was to have sex with his sister-in-law if she had not yet had any children and her husband had died. When Er died his younger brother whose name was Onan was requested by his father Judah to have sex with Tamar his sister-in-law and to give her a child. It is in verse 9 where it says, Onan knew the child wouldn't be his child so instead of ejaculating while he directly penetrated Tamar, Onan would pull out and ejaculate on the ground! This is the verse that people seek to distort and make it a sin to masturbate. But as you can see clearly form the scripture that Onan was not masturbating he was actually engaged in full sexual intercourse with his sister-in-law. The scripture also in no way implies that he committed a sin because he ejaculated on the ground. If anything Er's sin was the mistreatment of his sister-in-law through deception and not fulfilling his fathers instructions, which in turn set off a very bad sequence of events from that point on as a heritage for the whole line of his family.

Darrell L. Owens

When the detractors of masturbation seek to label masturbation
as a cause of dysfunction or irregularities in individuals and
society we know that there are a lot of things that can cause
dysfunction like; ones diet, smoking, irregular vascular health,
and our ability to manage stress. These are frequently the culprits
of the majority of societies dysfunctions by fact. No irony but no
one ever talks about the health benefits of masturbation. Doctors
and studies show that masturbation by itself can benefit a person
in many ways.

- **Masturbation is A Legitimate Option for Single
  Men and Women** – For those not seeking to take
  sexual risk in casual relationships or for one in a
  marriage with a partner who has no ability to sexually
  suit their husband or wife. It could be anything from an
  emotional disorder to erectile dysfunction. See
  masturbation.

- **Masturbation Can Improve Immune Function** –
  In men masturbation builds resistance to prostate glands
  becoming infected. In women it actually

builds her resistance to yeast infections. Masturbation can relieve painful menstruation and chronic back pain. It can to some degree reduce the chances of contracting transmitted diseases.

- **Masturbation is A Stress Reliever** – It can serve as a natural stress reliever and can increase concentration. It is well documented that sexual energy unattended or repressed hinders and retards one's focus. Masturbation can serve as a natural catharsis releasing enormous emotional and mental pressure especially thoughts and emotions associated with sex or sexuality! A Duke University study found that in order to get the maximum potential out of your sexuality one needs to have at least 200 orgasms a year! I don't think that realistically each of those orgasms can be had with a partner so masturbation would be a good resource in attaining that goal!

Darrell L. Owens

- **Masturbation is A Viable Option for Men and Women With No Suitor** – For those who have gone long periods of time without finding a suitable mate to actually have sex with! There are many, many people who struggle to connect with others for various reasons. They may have deep seeded esteem problems or may be extremely insecure. It be anything from their physical body and appearance to unresolved issues or being mentally or emotionally disturbed. Many men and women never find a mate to marry and begin to enter late years in life like their 50's and 60's and don't have a prospect in sight, masturbation is a very healthy practice and response to the building pressure of sexual energy stemming from being single and without a suitor.

Why People Lie & Cheat

To lie is to present false information as the truth, to cheat is to deceive something or someone. Both lying and cheating are synonymous and tied to one another. Lying is a simple form of cheating and cheating is a more elaborate form of lying. People almost never ask themselves why do I lie or cheat, they almost always ask why do others lie and cheat. Well they do it for the exact same reasons that you do it! If you really wanted to know the truth of why people lie or cheat you would have to start by being honest with your own self. If you want to write off all of the liars and cheaters in the world, you would probably have to off yourself. If you choose to only classify others as liars and cheaters you may need to check your mirror. If you choose to believe that people lie and cheat because they are just cold hearted you are seriously naive! Cheating's roots are found in economic poverty, emotional destitution, and intellectual deficiencies! Lying and cheating are social dysfunctions that come from personal non-development. This state of mind introduces fear in the heart, which then can causes an outbreak of lies and cheating! There is no chemical cure, nor punishment that can correct the behavior of lying and cheating. The only way to modify this behavior is through fairness, objectivity, and meeting fundamental needs in life like; equal opportunity, acceptance, and validation. People lie to avoid perceived or actual consequences and they cheat to conquer what they perceive in their mind as overwhelming challenges they can't win without some additional edge. These are the basic motivations for these behaviors. However, the deep and more underlying reason as to why people lie and cheat is the elephant in the room. Let me explain, the thing that gives lying and cheating it's appeal and makes it such a viable option as opposed to telling the truth is people don't do well with the truth, especially in relationships! Society in general, just doesn't prepare people to hear and deal with truth! We as a culture are not built mentally or emotionally in a way that we can process and respond to truth in a productive way.

Since we collectively know people don't do well hearing truth, it is that much harder to speak truth. In society it almost is never allowed, received, or appreciated when the truth is spoken. We work overtime trying to be politically correct so we don't damage people. Truth be told we shouldn't have to worry about damaging people by speaking the truth, but the reality is we do. There are no classes on how to hear truth and grow from it. As soon as we are born in the crib people start guarding us from truth as if it was to harsh and hurtful to say! See Children's drawings.

We don't want to hear truth, we don't want to have to speak it, and we don't dare tell ourselves the truth. We know how to be angry, we know how to lash out at people who tell us lies, but we have no idea how to constructively hear truth and respond to it productively! Can you see the kind of fix and complication this creates for all social interaction? If people lie and cheat on us we break, and if they tell us the truth that breaks us also.

So consequently we're in a position where we loose this way or we loose that way. We can't go left or right because we get broken coming and going. Consequently we choose to ignore and shy away from truth leaving ourselves at the mercy of our misconceptions about reality. All this leaves us in a place of insecurity, we don't trust each other, we don't trust ourselves, and we don't trust the truth. Then our trust issues become the perfect breeding ground for producing lies and cheating! When someone lies with you and for you it is duplicitous to be shocked if they turn around and lie to you! This is a bit technical and psychological but it is consequential for us to understand. People think when they lie for their mate or spouse the lying will be limited to others outside of the relationship. They never believe it will happen between the two involved in the relationship. It never occurs to them that they could become the object of each other's lies and cheating. The problem is, you can't just turn it off after indulging in it. The truth is if we lie with each other or for each other we are very apt to lie to each other! It is an inescapable problem that men and women remain blind to until it all comes out.

What happens when you lie and cheat for each other, subliminally what you tell yourself is there is justification for lying and cheating to each other, for the right reasons. This is the risk you run if you choose to operate in these kinds of practices with your relationship. Ultimately you can't control whether someone lie's to you or cheats on you, however there is something you can do that can be very productive during these very challenging moments. You can change your mindset and your approach towards the people you're in a relationship with in order to discourage any need for them to lie or cheat. Let me explain, you can remove the motivations your mate or spouse has to lie and cheat on you. This can be super effective because it changes the environment of the relationship. Which results in the relationship being overall safer! There is a certain kind of power and safety in removing a person's need to lie to you! This process requires you to remove the presence of any threat far from the heart of a person you love and believe you want to experience intimacy and happiness with!

Darrell L. Owens

Your relationship being under threat is not good because the mere thought of rejection or retaliation immediately engages the "lying dysfunction" inside the people you're in the relationship with. Lying is a learned defense mechanism people are often subliminally taught to resort too for many reasons. I am not asking you to accept abuse, mistreatment, or lies, but it is necessary for you to know the truth! You cannot get the truth if you become anxious and overreact and agitate a person to begin lying, this drives the truth further away from you! The truth helps you to understand and to respond out of insight and wisdom. This enables you to put people in the right places and spaces in your life it keeps you safe and them healthy! At the end of the day we know that there is really no human ability to defend against the offense of lying and cheating. Things are not always what they appear to be on the surface. You may feel good vibes and signs but still be blind to the complete picture of who a person is. We know that we can have all the facts and still not know the truth? Ask any good lawyer or judge. Lying and cheating often becomes a person's recourse in an attempt to mask their truth or their weaknesses.

So don't assume that what you see is the whole, when in fact it is only a part! Your challenge is to trust love more than you trust your intellect or other people. Love is the one; supernatural and superhuman quality that can level the playing field. It can safeguard your heart from those that may mean you no good! Love exposes the truth and the intent of those you are considering or already in a relationship with! For example there are people who are very passive in their deceit or dishonesty. They may not tell you anything but by not telling you anything they are telling you a lot! These people make it hard to realize what their truth is, but love will reveal their truth and expose their reality. The advantage love gives you with them is you don't have to know what they feel to know what you feel? If you never clearly understand what their angle is, love gives you the peace and wisdom to choose not to be occupied with that kind of mystery or potential confusion. Once you realize your truth, love helps you to bow out gracefully to experience liberty and personal empowerment. Turning to love is imperative, if you trust love to reveal truth you can eradicate the repetitive bad results you experience in your relationships by 70 or 80%!

Love is exceptional! It can negate the goal of over half of the lying and cheating you experience and can free you of the fear of being lied to and cheated on all together. It will free you of living guarded and shut up because you can't figure out who to trust. If you rework your thinking about the way you handle the people you're in love relationships with, love will change the game.

The Principle of "So Far"

I can't overstate the danger in "assuming" when it comes to love relationships. Or the gross negligence you engage in when you make commitments and decisions based on extremely limited knowledge. Assumption is basically making a determination and coming to a conclusion based on a few very small observations. My goal is not to guarantee that you will never experience failure in love relationships, but that you don't go through relationships and come out jaded, bitter, and worse off than you were. In a society so connected by rapid information sharing you can't survive dating and love by guessing, wishing, and assuming. You can't seriously investigate every action and hunch you feel, it will drive you insane. There are too many ways for your partner to cheat, sneak, and connect without you having a clue its happening. The methods are technical, untraceable, and quite efficient. If you allow it to, the stress will drag you into the dangerous waters of assumption and overreaction, which is nothing more than the torture chamber of fear!

This stress and fear will undermine whatever potential exist for you and the person you're in a relationship with. Learning not to assume the good or the bad will spare your relationship a lot of damage and increase your success with love and relationships. At a point you have to trust love, trust yourself, and let some opportunities be lost if that's what they are. In other words, let the chips fall where they damn well may fall! You stick with the truth or the proof. In the absence of proof you still have "your truth!" How you feel, how much you can take, and what you believe is fair! The beauty of the principle of "So Far" is, it pumps the brakes of your thoughts, emotions and reactions. So that your heart and mouth don't write a check that, won't add up when you check the balance of the relationship! The So far principle says, I really like you, "So Far." You make me feel amazing, "So Far." We've been out twice and talked everyday for three weeks it's been a blast and I more, "So Far"! You can't realistically and safely say that you "trust", "like", or "want" someone you just don't know! This is where we loose points and our ability to command respect! Respect doesn't come from men with a great checkbook or from women using their pussy in exchange for a commitment! Respect is given to the one who walks in wisdom and exercises self-control concerning fundamental matters in life. You meet somebody who holds your interest for three weeks they take you out twice and show you some attention and you say, "I'm falling in love". Six weeks and you say, they're my soul mate. By five months in we say, I can't live without them! This pathology is ridiculous because you don't have a clue of what you are talking about. The principle of "So Far" rescues you from this. This patience won't come natural to you because of what you're use to. If you rework your thinking on love and slow down enough to remember love has something to say if you want to hear it, you could really find someone special. The "So Far" principle gives love opportunity (time) to show you someone's truth. People won't just offer you their personal truth nor should they, their truth has to be drawn out by invitation and be waited out by love. Because love is in your corner and working to assist you in your relationship so you don't get blindsided by people who have lots of neatly dressed up issues or mean you no good. Take comfort in the safety that is the principle of "So Far."

Best Practices For a Healthy Relationship!

1. Know Your Self - Think of all the things we feed our minds and waste our intelligence on. We know everybody else's business, and all the latest drama on reality TV. But we don't know what we're allergic to, what our blood type is we don't even have a good list of our personal weakness in order to work on them. You need to know who you are and how you are! This is vital to your success and functionality in "any" relationship especially intimate ones. You need to know what your hot buttons are, what triggers your anger and what triggers your peace. You need to know what turns you on and what you really desire to do or not to do concerning relationships. Knowing yourself is key to; being the right person, attracting the right person, and handling those moments and people in the right way!

2. It's Only Potential - When you meet someone, regardless of what you feel or how he or she moves you in any one instance, they are nothing more than potential! You can't be willing to say I do or be willing to grant someone full access to your heart when you have no idea what or who he or she is! What you feel may be authentic to you but by no means should you rely on your feelings to make any significant relationship decisions! Your feelings are not qualified to decide if a person is good for you or not. Your feelings are void of that person's intent and true desire. They "may" be smart, disciplined, and honest, but they "may" be; crazy, aloof, or deranged! Your position is too let their actions and behavior tell you their truth. It is unwise and a sign of immaturity to agonize over the things you don't know, but it is healthy and very wise to respect what you do know! Until they have proven to you they are honest, without any ulterior motives, and genuinely interested they are just potential! You don't ask them to be these things you give them room to be or not to be these things. You may not know what or who they are initially but you know they're only potential so far!

3. Never Mind Your Feelings - Your feelings are temporary; they will leave as quickly as they come to you. They are fluctuating; they literally can swing from one extreme to the other daily! Your feelings are shallow and flippant; they are not designed to think critically. They're feelings don't follow them just feel them, and then put a period on their input concerning your relationship decisions. Whenever I talk about not catering to one's feelings I can literally feel people tuning me out subconsciously because culturally we are so conditioned to think, move, and operate according to our feelings it has become almost impossible to shut them off. Well, it my be difficult to do but if you are going to have success in love relationship you most certainly will need to NEVER MIND YOUR FEELINGS!

5. Look For Interest - Test their interest in getting to know you beyond the surface and superficial bases. Present them opportunities to spend time and hang out and see if they take advantage of them? If they rarely or never act on those opportunities this is a good way to tell they're not interested.

Remember, whether a person is interested or not, this should never become your gauge of your personal value and worth. A person's interest can be based off of a wide range of significant to insignificant factors. Employ your intuition you are not helpless when trying to survive people that are not interested in you. Measure their interest for yourself. If on a scale of 1-10 their interest in being in your presence and getting to know you personally is less than 7 they are not interested in you, not in an intimate way. This is not bad it's just a fact! Bow out gracefully! This play seems like a basic, something obvious to recognize but don't underestimate the power of your imagination to blind you to this when you are extremely interested in knowing them on a personal level. This point will be very effective in protecting you from those that mean you no good and would gladly take advantage of your interest in them!

6. Re - Negotiate Often - DON"T BE LOYAL TO A FAULT! At various points you need to "decide again" if going forward is best for you! This is supposed to be a self-loving and a private selfish moment for you.

You need to ask yourself again what you desire and are your needs being met? Take not to be afraid to ask these questions it is never your job to stay with someone for their need and not a mutual interest! You need to discern whether you're both at this new point are still suitable for one another? We taught you to keep hope alive but sometimes hope makes you blind to reality and you end up being loyal to your own detriment. Re-negotiation and asking yourself good questions can save you from wasting years of your life and living in regret. You have to stop doing things that don't work and be willing to lose to win!

7. Love Hard - Love is not sex nor is it a feeling! Love is acknowledgement and acceptance! If you love hard you will know the truth and accept it! Love is the revealer of human truth it is the missing link and the greatest gift of the divine to all of mankind. Loving hard is not a cliché, it is what you look like when you're mature and operate in wisdom when it comes to the various relationships in your life especially intimate love relationships.

Whether he or she is, good or bad, desirable or undesirable loving hard is all about being fearless in accepting hard human realities! Especially realities that don't line up with what your true desire is. Real love is your offense and defense when it comes to navigating hard intimate relationships it is the human power that tells you the things you wish you had known after you've wasted money, energy, and most of all time! Truly safest place is loving hard!

Rejecting Manipulation

Learning the difference between influence and manipulation is necessary to master social interaction with others. To be influential is to earn someone's trust through consistency and truthfulness of character. Manipulation is robbing a person in some clever, unfair, and unscrupulous way of their right to choose their own course of action. The idea that you don't have to accept certain aspects of reality, or that you can force reality to bend towards whatever you want it to be, is a very self-destructive perspective on life. Manipulation disrupts connection with others and drives good virtue out of your relationships. Manipulating your experiences is ill advised and will only prove to be a downfall rather than a key to success. There is zero chance that you can control other people successfully. No matter how weak-minded they may be, and no matter how good you think you are. Even if you were to gain sole control over an individual, it would only result in a devaluing of that individual in your eyes, and ultimately turn into some form of abuse.

The end result of a person giving you control over their life is you loose respect and desire for them. No matter how hard you try, it is not possible to desire or have a meaningful relationship with someone you don't respect. If you pay attention to human behavior you will find that people tolerate manipulation on certain levels and for limited amounts of time. When you are young and immature people will grant your manipulative request and respond to the fits you display. This is because your request is inconsequential. By granting your request makes no difference to anything or anyone. However, you will find that the older you get, the less people will be willing to withstand or entertain your manipulation, no matter how innocent or subtle it may be. This is the moment when society says: get it yourself! The moment everyone starts expecting you to perform without being coddled. No more catering to your fits, your wishes or your demands. This can be an uncomfortable awakening for a person who doesn't understand that you cannot realistically control other people. This moment feels like nobody cares and like the world is cold but it's the harsh reality of the rejection of manipulation.

Darrell L. Owens

The truth is, the older you get the more you're going to be held responsible for your own end. You're going to be challenged to build your own partnerships and relationships. You will have to prove your ability to operate fairly within a relationship. The more you try to manipulate and control the things and people around you, the worse the condition of your relationships will be. This is because people will not take kindly to a childish, manipulating adult. If you don't understand this early on you will be very perplexed even jaded by people's responses to your desire to befriend them, or to connect with them. Again, when you're young people will give you opportunities even if you are rife with manipulation. But as you grow older they will begin to say, "You had your opportunities," "what did you do with them?" It's hard not to be deceived by all of the manipulation we are bombarded by on a daily bases. You will have to find a way to see the truth, everyone who appears to be winning by manipulating people and things with their money, power or sex, are not winning! And at best, they are creating an illusion that will end in some form of pain or waste of valuable time.

Like all vices, manipulation is hard to stop doing once you've

started doing it. Manipulation may be one of the most

challenging things you will ever have to break yourself from.

When it comes to other people's choices; we literally can't stop

trying to control their affairs and decisions. It is vital for young

people to start cultivating the mindset to control only what they

can control. Then learn to allow things they cannot control to

exist and be. Things we do control like our bodies, our time, our

words and our choices. Are ours to control by God given right.

We don't have to pray for control or beg for it, these things were

given to our control. However, there are things we don't control.

Like rain or "time" its self. We can't change who our parents are

and we cannot change the past. We have to accept these things as

they are. We learn very early on the practice of controlling or

manipulating everything around us. This comes from the first

relationships we experience. We learn from our parents,

teachers, and our guardians the how to of manipulation. This is

where we embrace the idea that we can sway people and things

to be the way we want them to be.

We learn to push the right buttons, dangle the right bait, or use the right leverage to manipulate anything and anybody. With parents and their children this is a particularly bad idea. Parents should draw a clear line of difference between giving their children gifts vs. manipulating them with pleasures. Giving your child a gift for any reason should be a gift given and not a tactic to manipulate their behavior. There is a great difference between restricting a child from a privilege or a pleasure as a consequence of bad behavior vs. failing to communicate with them and gaining a real understanding of their mindset. Just to hold pleasure over their head to get an immediate compliance but no long-term correction is a tactic and it carries over into all of their other relationships. Parents many times are responsible for setting in motion the pattern within children to accept manipulation and to manipulate others. This produces a wrong belief in children that manipulation and submission are somehow love. When in fact manipulation is the opposite of love! As this process evolves at some point the manipulated, becomes the manipulator.

A cycle begins and you see manipulation at work now, in every aspect of our society. Politicians can't stay honest because of the standards set out to be a public official. Whenever the loss of power or position is at risk, this creates an environment where they can be manipulated. In every form of religion you have spiritual leaders condemning and manipulating their followers for personal gain. The same happens in friendships and partnerships, some people choose their friends or business partners based on who is willing to be manipulated. In intimate love relationships, a lot of people have tricked their way into a relationship by lying about their intent and their desires. This is to get a man or women to commit, after securing a commitment they attempt to further manipulate the relationship, not realizing that passion, nor fulfillment can exist where manipulation is the rule. Manipulation sabotages your relationships and is a form of witchcraft. Its only commodity is destruction and the state of being disturbed. It unfortunately is how we are conditioned to function in our relationships. The irony of the condition is, the manipulation we use to function, is exactly what makes us dysfunctional.

The point of living is being free to walk into the mystery of life with inquiry, suspense, and desire for what is new. It is not to control and manipulate others freedom! All people should be free to stay or leave, free to do right by you or to do you wrong. Free to tell you the truth or to lie to you. They can attract you, or drive you away. Setting others free "is" the power position for you! You're not setting them free to do whatever they want to in your life, you're freeing them to mess the whole thing up if they choose too. This way you remain safe, powerful, and uncompromised. Freeing others is the alternative to manipulation. It is your best and most effective tool in winning the game of relationship. Life and relationship should not be about making someone choose you, or taking away their ability to choose otherwise. If you can reject the temptation to manipulate within your relationship, you qualify to experience happiness in your relationship.

4 Potential Placements for People Who Come into Your Life

> **Friend/Close Confidant** - Some people are sent into your life because they just get you! This is not a sign that they're your soul mate or a sex partner! Their ability to empathize and be in touch with how you feel is obvious; this comes with the gift of friendship. They demonstrate all the characteristics that make them trustworthy. They learn from you and teach you as well. They don't want anything from you except your good, and the same in return. They may not do it for you romantically or you may not do it for them, once you, or both of you have decided on engaging in a sincere friendship take sex off the table, you've found a perfect candidate for a friend or confidant. Don't misplace these people in your life and miss the blessing that friendship brings!

> **Partner for a Common Goal** - Some people come into
your life and they share your passion for a cause or
perhaps a business venture. They were sent for business,
common passions, and as connections to your next step.
It is vital that you recognize this and place them in the
correct position in your life. They may think they want
to be with you romantically, or want to sleep with. They
may believe they want to be your friend but if they are
meant to be a partner for a common goal you have to
recognize it and keep that in mind. If you listen closely
and don't misinterpret the connection you sense and rush
to jump into the bed with them or by place them in some
other wrong position in your life, you may have found
the partner, the key or the connection to your success
and your dreams. If you don't try and force people to be
something that they aren't in your life, life is much
sweeter.

➤ **Distant Associate** - Some people you can readily identify that you are not interested in them and their not interested in you. They add no value to you at all. They don't want to be your friend and you don't want them as a friend. You may know of him or her and they might see you everyday but there is no cause or connection nor reason for interaction! Do not introduce unfounded tension into these interactions nor towards these people, you have no dog in a fight with them. Some people are just in the same building as you are, others are just in the same city as you and others are just on the same planet as you! Know these people and don't misplace them in your life!

> ➤ **Romantic Interest** - These are people you meet and immediately your interest is peaked? They are somewhat captivating either with their style and presence or their mind and strength. Once you actually meet them and get the chance to chop it up with them and have been sensitive enough to discern that they don't belong in any of the other first 3 places and you feel right about exploring them further they should be placed in the "Romantic Interest" column. Then immediately see my chapter on **"Best Practices for a Healthy Relationship!**

5 Ways to Get a Good Man and Keep Him

1. Be Rational

Ladies men have a need to make sense. You must be able to communicate the facts and do it with sound reasoning. Choosing to be rational and less emotional shows a man your wisdom and makes you extremely valuable even more attractive. Nothing makes a man start thinking about forever like a rational sound thinking woman. Your man wants your passion, your emotion, and your insight, but you must give it in the right way. Show your man that you want to be with him. Show him that you know how to talk to him and touch him. It won't always be easy but the trouble of remaining rational even when you feel like loosing it will pay off big time! Don't let your emotions control the outcome of your relationship with a man you truly do love and desire. If the relationship doesn't succeed and if you both ultimately go your separate ways let it be for real reasons and not because you emotionally tore down your own intimate love life!

2. Be Teachable

No man is interested in a woman he has no influence over or a woman he can't teach anything to. If you truly feel like a man can't teach you anything you probably should bow out of the relationship gracefully. To remain in a man's life who you can't learn from or take his counsel on the choices and challenges that transpire in your life breeds; distrust, disrespect, and offensive behavior over time. This produces his response of frustration, recklessness, and anger to the smallest of things. No man wants a woman who knows everything. Don't assume you know what your man wants. Don't assume he is like any other man ever, because he is not! He will tell you exactly how he wants to be touched, handled, and kept. When you assume that he is like every, or any other man you treat him like that! Appeal to his manhood with regard and respect. Acknowledge his greatness and what attracted you to him most. Maintenance his base nature with sex, food, and money but don't define him by those or define your relationship with him through those things. To be teachable will require some level of submission to your man and the risk of you being vulnerable to him.

If he isn't worth the a risk or the trouble of submitting to, you should definitely be moving on to the next one.

3. Shut Up

Ladies this does not mean that your wrong, it doesn't mean that he didn't hear you or that you didn't get your point across, it doesn't mean you're his slave or less than it just means shutting up in certain moments will help your man! You say I want it to work well; there is no "it" without him. You say why should I be quiet for him? Because your words are getting in the way of his sound reasoning, your man always hears you. A wise woman knows that she doesn't need to see a certain behavior from her man before she stops arguing. She's patient and confident in the truth that he is silently self-correcting and this attitude will work in her favor. This is how a wise woman handles her man but a foolish woman goes word for word and toe to toe all the time, this is not good. Ladies another woman can't take him, her sex cant move him, but you and a slick mouth will tear the whole damn thing down. You are going to literally usher him into the arms of another woman.

4. Love The Inch

Love the inch, cherish the inch, most women take the inch that a man gives them all the while dreaming about the mile. They get the man's attention by inch standards accepting exactly what he chooses to give them. Then when he gives them the relationship they switch the game up and put mile responsibilities on him because now you think you've got him where you want him. However ladies taking a mile will run him away! Love him and be content with the inch until he gives you the mile. Let him know, I don't want to take anything from you that you don't want to give me? Say this with your actions not your words! If he doesn't move soon enough and you know in yourself its time for you to move on, don't even talk about it bow out gracefully and be on to the next one! But to try and force him to give something he is not offering you, will be a disaster. You may say, "I don't care, he needs to do better or get out," please understand, that when you put him out, another woman and the next girl will literally pull around the corner and toss his bags in the truck and take him home saying, I'll take the inch!

5. Study Your Man

Be a student of your man, you have never seen this man before. You can't take your mother's or your sister's advice on him. Someone else's idea about how to handle man is deeply contaminated with, their own judgment, weaknesses, and unique circumstances. None of which apply to the man sitting in front of you. I don't care if you read a study on 10,000 men those studies would show what is true with the 10,000 men studied. Your man wasn't in the study. If he can have his own fingerprint, not one identical, he can have his own experiences and a personality that you cant duplicate or predict! Study your man, the one you lay with, talk to, and play with. He is not some fictitious character out of the movies or your soap opera, study him, you have a front row seat! Understand him, and remember understanding is not just about what he did, but "why" he did it! Study his temperament and his character to know how you should touch him and support him. This is what will give you an advantage at spending forever with him!

5 Ways to Get a Good Woman and Keep Her

1. Make Her Safe & Secure

First, cause her to trust you. Then protect her trust. Don't ask her if she loves you? Ask her if she feels safe? She must be emotionally safe, financially safe, physically and relationally safe and secure. If your girl's heart safely trust in you she has the power and the will to help you manifest every dream and venture God has put into your heart! You will be amazed at her performance in your life when her heart, safely trust you.

2. Confront and Overcome your Own Fears and Insecurities

Your girl may not know what happened to you or be able to comprehend the toll it took on you but she will clearly see its affects and feel it in the way you treat and handle her. So you have to confront every issue you have and deal with it. If not she will find it, she will expose it, and it will become a source of conflict. She will know that it is either retarding you, and you're to weak overcome it, or that it will exist as a potential force to be turned on her, and that she could become the object of the blunt force of your dysfunction.

3. Listen to Your Girl

Even if you don't get it, listen. What she is saying and what she is trying to say will be two totally different things. If you listen real close she is saying something that you need to hear. Something that will make you able to protect, nourish, and build her. To ignore her only sets the atmosphere for her to talk to someone else she perceives as strong, compassionate, and willing to listen. She will either talk to you, or to someone else! She needs to say it and you need to hear it. Your woman is trying to tell you something but has no clue how to communicate it in a way that you can hear it. Listen to her, then tell yourself "I heard what she said" and then let love reveal what else she could be trying to say. In other words don't just listen, listen twice!

4. Get Some Money

You don't have to rob, steal, or sell out to get money but you got

to get it! Men are created to earn perform, and dominate. Every

man can and must do it. Simplify your life by putting away

childish things, silly women, and the things you know to be

distractions. Focus on what is important. Then when you make

money, manage your money, then your money will multiply.

Once this happens a good woman won't even want your money,

she'll just want to share your dreams with you. She wants the

money to be a means to an end for you both.

5. Provide for Her, Utilize Her, and Celebrate Her

Your girl has needs, they're not just material or tangible ones.

She needs to be validated, affirmed, and confirmed! If your girl

needs a listening ear, you listen. If she needs attention, you bring

her some. She needs to be utilized in your world. Find a way,

incorporate her into what you do. She can add value and make a

difference for you both! Celebrate her, don't let anyone speak

more highly of her than you do. Highlight all her strengths and

strengthen all her weaknesses, you will get her and keep her!

Dating Wisdom for Those 25 and Younger

I intend on raising your success rate about 50% through what I call reworked wisdom. These principles will help you navigate the fierce waters of love and connection safely. It is not impossible to find true love while young, however this season of your life is made of "vintage moments." These moments are the times when you're in your prime, at your greatest strength, vigor, and opportunity for success. This is not the time to be closed minded, or to settle. This is the time for you to explore your reality, a time to rouse your imagination, and to practice setting goals and achieving them. This time in your life should be filled with interaction, the ones that befall you and those you get in the way of! You should be establishing your heart, overcoming your fears, getting confortable with the mystery of your journey. Build your character, feed your mind, and sort out your worldview and your convictions about God. Take these points as guides in love relationships when you're 25 and younger!

Darrell L. Owens

- **Speak Two Languages** – All relationships have two distinct forms of language and communication. One is verbal and one is behavioral. You must learn to communicate and receive from both mediums of communication. Remember when people in a relationship aren't saying anything, they are saying a lot!!! What people do or don't do will reveal desire, thoughts, and intent! What you say or don't say can technically be held and used against you at any time. However, The interesting thing to remember is, people many times don't say what they really mean, and they don't know what they really want! This is why you need to be able to communicate behaviorally as well and verbally. Don't just read what they are saying read what they are doing! Then you are to rely on the power of your love. Remember that judgment and pressure drive people into hiding but the acceptance and freedom of love draws them out! Love has something to say to you if you want to hear it!

142

- **Remember Distance Is Your Friend** – Having and not having the right distance in your relationship can make a person your lover or your enemy! People need room to make good decisions. Shysters prey on people who don't insist on having room to make their decision. We all need room to get it right or to get it wrong. Room to be honest or room to be dishonest, because if you're living in prisoner mode your life is most miserable! There are those who have hit the relational lottery because one works at night, and the other works during the day. The proper distance sponsors health in a relationship. The couple has different work schedules but they aren't being cheated. They have to schedule free time and family events but this isn't some form of self-inflicted pain. They have to be deliberate about their plans and make the most of the moments they have with one another. We would all be better if we were more engaged in the "now moments" of our lives. If the two in the relationship were to even work on the same schedule, it would still be wise to be deliberate at giving each other the right amount of space to thrive. Distance is your friend.

- **Be as Mobile as Your Cell Phone** – In this season you should explore, experience, and establish yourself. You should be fully taking in the affects and meaning of your various experiences. You should be establishing real friendships and understandings.

You should be testing your character, your level of endurance, and cultivating your personal faith in God! Being locked in and tied to a serious relationship in this season of your life is not wise simply because you are in the stage of discovery and learning. Between 15 -25 be committed to yourself and your own development. Get in tune with the process of life. It is very important that you understand how people, money, business, and faith work! Remember that there is a process to everything. Knowing and understanding what comes next after a particular experience is essential to getting safely and happily to your destiny or destination. The point here is to "get there" and to get there in good emotional and mental health!

To engage in a serious committed relationship at this point is kind of like putting the cart before the horse. It may not be impossible to find true love and a suitable mate before age 25 but think about it, in this season you have so many things about yourself, the world, and God you don't know but you believe you know this other person is the right one for you, at this point? Finding Mr. or Mrs. Right in this season is arbitrary and non-essential and to make this experience priority probably will not serve you well! You need to stay as emotionally, spiritually and mentally mobile as possible!

There are many experiences besides the "love relationship" that you will need to experience and reconcile! Focus on the journey and all it comes to teach you along the way. Explore, Explore, Explore, and stay mobile!

- **Remember Friendship Is a Foundation** – The first building block that needs to be established for success in relationships is friendship. Before you become intimately involved with or committed to another person, you would do yourself a favor to have 2 or 3 good friends. Preferably of the opposite sex, ones you definitely are not sexual with, and friends that have made an open commitment to be a friend and you theirs. Having friends that you share an open vulnerable safe bond with opens the way for the kind of personal development that a person cannot find in their rearing, in school or in the arms of a lover!

  Your family and your friends are your supports, resources, and true wealth. These are the people you should be using in your life to meet your emotional, psychological, and social needs. What friendship does for an individual in love relationships is what college does for an individual in life it prepares them to have success.

The preparation for a intimate relationship is not the job of a boyfriend or a girlfriend, that is inadvisable and a bad way to learn a lot of necessary lessons that make us socially healthy.

- **You Gotta Keep A Secret** – When I speak of keeping a secret I am directly referring to two people in the early stages of dating resisting the urge to put their new potential relationship on a table for family, friends, or associates to; assess, give opinion or attack.

First of all it is not good in general to just freely offer up what you are into or doing period. The same principle your mother would teach you about keeping your money in your pocket alerting you to the dangers of flashing it, don't do it! Like flashing your money can attract bad attention and invite harm to you so does telling people what's happening between you and your new friend. It attracts comment, critique, and chatter that can potentially hurt your opportunity for happiness.

Darrell L. Owens

When you hear people who try to make you feel bad in some way for keeping your relationship status off the table, kindly but shrewdly check them and request that they move on from the conversation. This is because I promise you that the person who is prying in to this aspect of you life is a generally problematic person who probably doesn't do well with a lot of people because they have been betrayed and crossed for always opening their mouth! Remember the principle of keeping your business to yourself is a principle of safety across the board in life. Privacy and deception are not the same thing! People tend to treat privacy as if you're hiding something under board. As if keeping a secret is somehow sinister, this is not the case. One of the main dangers in telling your business to other people is, they often immediately start trying to form your view and opinion to theirs! In other words they're going to tell you who is good and not good for you.

148

They don't have your insight or point of view, they won't employ the same amount of consideration that you will, because people always treat other people's things far worst than they do their own and you can count on that! For balance I am focusing on the initial or early stages of the relationship. Let me give you a time frame that can represent the early stages. The early stage is as long as it takes for you both to get a firm understanding of each other and what each of you is looking for, that may take some time but there is no rush. This process does not always require you to directly engage a person, just flow with the moments and sit back and let their actions speak. When their actions speak then love will speak and you will have insight to make good decisions for yourself and all involved. Remember you have to speak both languages and trust love to guide you!

- **Carry Your Own Weight** -There is a certain temptation that you should be aware of, it is the temptation to begin leaning the weight of your life on someone new or a potential love interest. It is possible to weigh people down with your personal problems way to early in the relationship! No one and I mean absolutely no one goes out looking for someone to carry!

So you won't have good luck with finding a person that wants to carry you without abusing you.

People initiate relationships to share themselves with someone and to have companionship. People are looking for someone to walk life out with, not for! When you meet someone interested in getting to know you, the last thing you want to do is start, introducing issues. You don't want to appear to nor should you actually need them to ponder, answer for, or to rescue you from anything. After a short time it may be in order to share honestly if your dealing with something significant but along with that confession and moment of sharing, it is vital to demonstrate a healthy and strong sense of understanding of where you are and what it means for you as it pertains to your next step and future. In other words don't even mention any frivolous issue that may arise in your life. Don't look to them to assist you with anything on a personal level. It is inappropriate; it is a sign of desperation and worse of all it reeks of weakness. If you have to say time out for the day do it. If it means time out for the weekend, or for now period, do what you need to do but by all means, do not lay the burden of taking care of your personal issues on someone new coming into your life. If you need to borrow money; or you have a flat tire, maybe you need an emergency ride, or just to vent and talk to someone, turn to the people you've already established a relationship with. The first question you and everyone else should be asking is, who was the go to person for these things before I, or they existed! This question is important because it puts things into right perspective. If you're an adult working and living everyday there should be healthy relationships already forged around you to cover these kinds of things.

When you meet a person who doesn't have any solid relationships outside of you, it's probably best to run the other way! This speaks very little of their individual exceptionalism! They're probably not friendly, they probably don't help others, and most likely are not productive or resourceful individuals!

It is a dagger in the heart of a person's respect for you when you show up and within a two-week period you begin dumping weight and responsibilities for your existence on them. Just make sure when preparing to date someone, all of your bases are properly covered! Leaving you and a new intimate love interest to just getting to know each other's character and personal exceptionalism! Carry your own weight.

Marriage ReWorked

Darrell L. Owens

The Madness of Marriage

Marriage as we know it is failing, because it is based on a premise that disregards individualism, exceptionalism, and personal liberty! The idea that in order for two people to experience intimacy, unity, and agreement they must disregard these things is in fact madness! The fathers who shaped marriage did so according to their limitations, they could not see the effect time, progress, and change would have on the tradition of marriage. These men did not realize the implications of an evolving culture. Once marriage became an institution instead of a relationship, it became stuck and in constant decline. Marriage for most has become a point of struggle and vexation. Most people only appease the institution out of respect for its intended purpose. There are people who think the institution of marriage is fine as it is, they believe it's just the people in the marriage that are flawed.

They would rather question the character of the people in the marriage instead of questioning the model of marriage itself. People would like to blame the decline of marriage on a rouge and ungodly culture, but what's really undermining marriage is an expanding culture! It's not a workplace fling or a weekend rendezvous that is derailing these unions, it is when men and women refuse to expand or consider new ways of approaching the covenant of marriage. Marriage in its current model is either broken or at least a bygone relic of a time that has surely passed! Men and women of the 21st century may regard marriage, but not its application because its been proven to be inconsistent with modern culture! When I speak of modern culture, I am speaking of the better part of the last 75 years. Whenever a modern man or woman experiences the current model of marriage it carries more burden than beauty!

I am not against marriage, however I don't believe that the model is adequate, or helpful in a modern generation. Sometimes it feels like we are setting people up to fail. Whenever we sit back and allow the same obvious and bad decisions to be made over and over again. Specifically I am speaking of individuals who get married for God's sake and not their own sake! Those who believe they ought to marry because of pregnancy. Or those who are under the false impression that marriage is God's ordain path to happiness in life. It's about time that we stop perpetuating these myths and ways of thinking. There is far too much damage being leveled through these decisions for us to keep saying try it again that way and trust God more. People who believe in the current model of marriage without objectivity are in my opinion, very dangerous. These people constantly attempt to hang and re-hang this model of marriage around the necks of new generations of young people.

Who are completely confounded by the incompatibility of marriage and life today! These diehard traditional marriage supporters try to force modern couples to have a traditional marriage or a biblical marriage. I find this very bizarre and it raises a flag for me when such disregard is in play concerning individuals. Teaching and learning have been around as long as marriage has, both in the world and in the bible but you don't here anyone walking around saying everyone needs a traditional education or a biblical education! Education has taken steps and evolved both how we teach and what we see as relevant to be taught! So why with marriage do we refuse to evolve? To ask a couple from 2029, to experience marital success with a marriage model from 1929, would be ridiculous. The couple from 2029 is at such a disadvantage by culture, options, and experiential knowledge. A modern couple in a marriage can't apply biblical doctrine to their marriage because the marriage isn't a biblical marriage.

They can't apply traditional reasoning to the marriage because the marriage isn't a traditional marriage! This is putting new wine into old wineskins and it doesn't work! It won't work because the modern couple has a "modern and indigenous" marriage, which puts it out of the reach of the principles of the old and current model. The old principles for marriage are not compatible with the practices of today. When we try to apply old practices to a new generation's mindset it's like the wine and the wineskins in Jesus' teachings, it's going to break and ruin both individuals involved. Our great grandparents used an outhouse as a bathroom. Think about this for a moment, that generation did not view the outhouse as cruel, less than, or as a living hell. They were conditioned and possessed the grace to handle the outhouse and could deal with it in a way that this generation could not. If you ask people who were married 90 years ago who were in a different time, and of a different mind. They would tell you that their options and limitations were strong factors in their decisions to, stay in or to leave their marriages.

A lot of them today would tell you that there were circumstances that determined their decisions to get married and stay married, and it wasn't because they were seeking to do it God's way. It was in a different culture and they had a completely different set of circumstances than we do today! I remember speaking to a man who had been married over 30yrs and as I was going through my own marital breakdown and eventual divorce he gave me some advice that both caught me off guard and stole some respect I had for him. His advice was to let my wife think she was right and in control then do whatever I was going to do anyways. I felt like Jesus' disciples must have felt when they said , who in their right mind would want to get married then? Let me say, I believe in monogamy and the benefit it brings to our social and human existence, but I have no faith in the traditional model of marriage that so many of our couples have fallen victim to. This is not conjecture; the proof is in the facts! The first thousand years of church history teach us that marriage was not a Christian sacrament or institution.

Marriages between couples was established and sanctioned by

the two being married and their families. They didn't receive

sanctioning or the blessing of the church or religious leaders! It

was the Christians of the Roman Catholic Church that began the

shift of marriage and it's ordination from personal and familiar

to the hands of civil governments. This was reinforced by

Christians of the Protestant Reformation that broke away from

the Catholic Church over disagreements about doctrine.

Marriage was initially a contract between the marriage partners

only, but once marriage was recognized as a sacrament of the

church it got entangled in spiritual protocols, conflicts and

emotionalism. Like the Book of Common Prayers produced by

the Anglican Church along with it's most popular prayer to date.

We call it the marriage vows this prayer was introduced into the

protestant church and is still sworn by today as if it were

scripture. However this prayer is not in the bible or inspired by

God at all, real men created it! The point I am making is; there is

progression and growth constantly happening to our idea of

marriage that demands constant expansion to our idea.` If we

say, God ordains marriage fine, but we can't say He ordained a particular form, method or model of marriage. Adam & Eve are a model of marriage but God never ordain it as "the" model. Jacob, David, Solomon, and Gideon are a model of Jewish/Christian Polygamy but God never ordained it as "the" model of marriage. These models were unique to their time and culture and it is irresponsible to force modern marriages into the Adam and Eve or a David and Solomon model. If we watch the "Motion of things," they either organically, or intelligently evolve or grow, but change is inevitable! You see this with technology, how we communicate, our medicine, music, and our machines. When Thomas Edison invented the record player he had no clue that in the fullness of time a Steve Jobs would introduce the iPod! The point was music, and music is still the point! But who knew what the future held by way of evolution of the model or method by which we get that music? There is nothing more frustrating than to watch those we love be humiliated and crushed by a dysfunctional system that doesn't have to be. The men, the women, and the children devastated by this system of marriage that doesn't work is disheartening and its all because it's comfortable and all we have known.

If this generation is going to embrace and benefit from marriage at all, the model must be allowed to change and evolve. This will no doubt mean relieving marriage of it's monopoly on happiness and the wrong belief that one model of marriage is God's preferred and righteous way.

The Confusion Of A Beautiful Covenant

The original idea of marriage was simple and straight forward. It did not have the psychological, spiritual, and emotional confusion we experience from it today. People have looked to marriage as the foundation and the undergird of society and our happiness. However, this is not realistic or sustainable. Marriage was a simple minded act that produced some basic benefits such as, companionship and physical company. Marriage was less poetic but it was very practical. Two people could come together and have companionship, procreation, and security minus the kind of drama we experience in marriage today. The idea of marriage shifted from a simple one to a very fanciful and shallow one. This shift was a defining and a detrimental one for the institution of marriage. When fantasy and ceremonies were introduced to marriage relationships it made them complex and produced many images that threaten every marital union even to this day.

These images have a powerful effect on our thoughts and decisions in the dating stage. They're often based on a few encounters and conversations. Operating from images of people and from images of your relationship is problematic because the image is based off very little reality and a lot of internal fantasy. When our images of a person and our relationship is confronted by reality it is shocking, disheartening, and painful. In our culture image is king. The idea of marriage is literally loaded with tons of images that just aren't true in reality. For instance the notion that personal happiness can be found in another person, false! The idea that God gives a special blessing to those who marry verses those who don't, false! Or the notion that sacrifice is proof of love, or that there is a, "right one" for you sent by God, false and false! These are just a few examples of how our convictions are shaped by our perceptions and images. The point is, these images about marriage and God don't ring true in reality. When a person seeks to live their life based only on images of life rather than the realities of life you get the success and fail rate of marriage we have today.

When two people get married it is important that the two of them be firmly grounded in reality. Because living in an upscale neighborhood and in a high-class house won't change or erase trust issues and fear. It won't add love or understanding to a relationship and no matter how much the image promises it, happiness will elude the union! Whether we care or not may be a totally different story, however, it is well documented that in a marriage people can only: mask and hide their truth but for so long and at some point the truth emerges whether you're ready or not. Then you're forced to deal with what is and not what was projected through the image! If you desire to be married or if you're actually in the process of getting married you need to deal with your own attachment to your images of marriage or else. The idea that God has linked marriage and falling in love together is created by men. It is false, confusing, and dangerous! Mainstream Christians act as if marriage can only be considered if two people meet and fall in love when the truth is, marriage and falling in love isn't like a hand and glove, or a head and hat, they're not a perfect match!

This kind of thinking does a lot of harm to innocent people just seeking to have an intimate, monogamous love relationship. This belief has done far more harm than good and has put pressure on people to; seek to get married in order to fall in love or to fall in love to get married! I am not saying falling in love is evil nor am I saying it is impossible. I am not saying that marriage should be banned! But I am saying, pairing marriage with falling in love is the devil in the details! The notion of falling in love is often hoped for but is it helpful? I have never heard a person ask the question, "How do I fall in love?" Because on a deep level they know that there is no way to make ones self fall in love. And even if they could, then how do I make the other person fall in love back? This presents a serious question to the relationship; are they willing to accept the truth when it is revealed or will they engage in manipulation and seek to force the relationship to be what they desire for it to be? The belief that marriage and falling in love are synonymous pushes people into a place were they feel pressured to fabricate feelings in a relationship that just don't show up in reality!

This pressure does not allow a person to be honest with others nor does it allow them to truthfully regard their own feelings about the relationship or the other person! Sexual suppression is a great adversary to the union of marriage. Sex should never be used to leverage or force marriage onto individuals. The tie that binds and says sex belongs exclusively only in marriage has forced countless men and women into making bad, negligent, and disastrous decisions to marry. Any integral teacher, doctor, or therapist will admit that this is dangerous. Because when you encounter people with sexual frustration and suppression, you find a group of individuals who are not thinking clearly ie. Catholic Priest and young boys! Both the woman and the man's decision-making faculties are often impaired! Likely resulting in failure, what we call marriage today. All this adds a whole different level of pressure on any person to get married and to make that far-reaching decision sooner than later with a high degree of recklessness! This is the pathology that introduces force and manipulation at the on set of the marriage. Because of desperation, people will give anything or do anything to close the deal!

These attitudes of force and manipulation often remain as reoccurring characters throughout the extent of the marriage! It is not advisable and it is not healthy in any way to utilize force and manipulation within any relationship especially marriage, it will be destined to fail! Being stuck in a marriage filled with force and manipulation has a special kind of misery that puts a person in distress and makes them dangerously desperate for peace. The truthful and cultural motivations for getting married don't align with the fantasy we market marriage as today. People truthfully got married for money and land not for love and emotion. People got married to create alliances with neighboring villages not because of a need for connection. People got married to divide the responsibilities of labor, not to share their lives together with another. People didn't choose whom they wanted to marry up until the 15th century and certainly God wasn't choosing their spouse to be. People had both multiple wives and multiple husbands but women never held authority period.

People married to secure land and property for children as legal airs, via decent, not for caring and sharing with on another.

People got married by sexual intercourse and a financial payment, not by; ministers, ceremonies, rings, and for love. People began to go to the church to get married because of the church fathers belief that they needed to control what people were doing especially concerning sex not because it was "Holy Matrimony"! The truth about what actually motivates people to get married verses the fantasy we use to sell the idea of marriage are two very different things. The confusion ensues when you advertise marriage as one thing but in application it's a whole other thing. Connection should come naturally it shouldn't involve labor and work! It should not be characterized by so much confusion. It should not be work to like the one you're married too. We should not have to make a yeoman's effort at being married everyday, to have to give max effort to listen to a spouse talk or to share their feelings in general.

Darrell L. Owens

This is silent torment and secret agony . To be forced to
celebrate with someone without any thrill and without desire, is a
form of suffering. This makes the heart callous and it builds up
hostility towards the other spouse! Then dysfunction happens,
you try to pretend and convince yourself that you're in love
when you're not, you try to feel something that you just don't.
It's the confusion of a beautiful and simple covenant that could
all be solved by love and the realities it reveals.

Biblical Marriage vs. Traditional Marriage

Marriage is complex because we aren't really sure what marriage is. We know what they tell us to assume marriage is but we don't know the truth. So literally with each generation marriage gets more and more obscure and confusing especially as men try to use the bible to define it! All scripture is profitable for correction and instruction in righteousness but what does the bible really say about marriage? The bible mentions people who were married; and it speaks of God being married to His people, and even states the fact that sometimes marriages end in divorce! Yet, the bible has almost nothing to say about the proactive act of getting married in the first place. With this in mind, it would be better to say marriage should be based on biblical principles rather than saying, one should have a "biblical marriage". Biblical and traditional marriage are two totally different things. Let me explain, a biblical marriage would be, a marriage utilizing the practices of the bible. If you know what those practices were, no one really wants a biblical marriage!

A marriage based off of biblical principles would be to take truths that apply to friendship and brotherhood, and apply them accurately within the marriage covenant! You will hear religious charlatans declaiming the idea of "Marriage" with great fervor and attempting to establish it and define it within the confines of the bible, but still they don't practice the marriage we find in the bible. Biblical marriage meant male ownership, women were like chattel and often equated with land or livestock Dt. 20:5-7 / Ex. 20:17. "Thou shalt not covet thy neighbor's house, wife, slave, ox or donkey". Biblical marriage was polygamous marriage where men could have as many sexual partners as they could afford. King Solomon alone was recorded to have had over 700 wives and 300 concubines 1 Kings 11:3. Abraham, Isaac, Jacob and Judah, all had multiple wives or concubines! Biblical Marriage said if a woman's husband died before having children, then his brother was expected to marry the widow or wives and the woman was required to submit to him sexually and bare children to continue the brother's lineage. This is what was called "Levirate marriage" from the Latin word levir meaning brother-in-law. Gen. 38:6-10, Deuteronomy 25:5-10. Biblical

Marriages could only take place if the spouses were of the same faith and ethnicity Ezra 9:12. These commandments were the grounds that some racist would use to suggest and say that black and white's shouldn't marry! Biblical Marriages required the woman to be completely subordinate to the man. The implicit biblical meaning was less than and lower than the man in Ephesians 5:22. Biblical marriage wasn't based on love or affection, and how you felt certainly did not matter. The woman had no say in this process; she was her father's to give away through arranged marriage Genesis 2:24. Biblical Marriage required that if a man raped a virgin girl he had to pay her father 50 shekels of silver and the girl/victim was required to marry her rapist Genesis 22:28-29! Biblical marriage was only valid if the bride was a virgin. If she was not, then she was to be executed literally stoned to death Duet. 22:13-21. Biblical Marriage endorsed marrying your slave or POW after conquering an enemy's camp and taking the women and children hostage! As concubines the women and the children were your property to do as you pleased. This was a valid biblical form of marriage.

Biblical Marriage wasn't high on Jesus' list, Jesus chose not to marry, Jesus largely warned against it and encouraged his disciples to abandon household in order to follow him (Matthew 19:29; Mark 10:28-30; Luke 9:57-62). While you hear Jesus talking indirectly about marriage but directly about divorce and adultery it is only right to state that Jesus never got married himself and even seemed to discourage it. It is also important to remember that Jesus' perspective of marriage was not the same as our perspective of marriage today! This is because, whenever Jesus mentioned marriage He was referring to biblical marriage and when we refer to marriage, our point of reference is traditional marriage. The apostle Paul also remained unmarried and taught marriage only as a concession to those unable to keep their sexual urges in check. Paul likewise encouraged male believers: "Do not seek a wife" (1 Corinthians 7:27) Think about it, if neither Jesus nor Paul preferred marriage nor for their followers, why do some Christians maintain that the bible enshrines biblical marriage as the blessed way to coexist? Traditional marriage has no biblical sacraments and no factual declarations about God desiring everyone to get married!

Traditional marriage is in fact a social construct and is what lots of mainstream Christians like to teach new couples about and call it biblical when in truth there is not very much biblical about traditional marriage, yet people use the Christian scriptures to try to validate traditional marriage. These two versions of marriage are not the same! Biblical marriage is obviously the kind of marriage we actually find in the bible. Traditional marriage is what we actually practice and experience today. However, traditional marriage is between one man and one woman, this isn't biblical. The documents of scripture are more than implicit in their support of Israelite men having multiple wives as many as they could reasonably support. God participating in bringing these unions together and His blessing on these polygamous marriages in the bible doesn't help the one man and, one-woman argument. In spite of popular thought, not one single biblical book states or substantially supports that marriage must be between one man and one woman! Traditional marriage is accomplished through the process of a ceremony this isn't biblical. Traditional marriage is till death do you part and this is not biblical.

Traditional marriage is a partnership, a team venture equal across the board, and this to is not biblical. They say traditional marriage is the specific model that provokes God's blessing but we know that this is not biblical! Traditional marriage gets presented under biblical authority, then labeled American and patriotic, and at the same time assumed that it comes with God's choicest blessings. How could it not be God's idea and the only way to prosper? It is not a new ploy for men to use religion and the bible to control the masses by playing on their natural need for connection and companionship. These people function off of others dysfunctions. These same people take the bible literally when it works for them, but when you show them something in the bible they don't endorse in the same black and white document, they reject the bible and stand on their own fanciful interpretations. They perceive change as a loss of principle and purity. They are hypocrites and opportunist who have no interest in the prosperity of the whole! And of course in their minds the masses don't love God and are going to hell anyways! History tells us that marriage in the world has been progressively influenced by culture and spiritual enlightenment!

The idea that we can use old interpretations and clichés based on scripture to assist modern couples with options and different problems that weren't present years ago, is what gives us the staggering statistics on divorce, abuse, and remarriage we have today! Marriage has always been introduced and shrouded in fantasy, faith, and romance which can be misleading. It is important that we make the concept of marriage clear. Marriage is very human and a very risky and earthy concept. We have to take in what we experience, and respect what those experiences teach us as we walk forward into this mystery of life and connection called marriage. Marriage cannot address our personal dysfunctions. Those dysfunctions must be resolved and healed by wisdom and self-correction! Better principles about marriage will set us free from seeking happiness from our marriage, rather than bringing happiness with us, and sharing that happiness with another in a marriage. The challenge of having to make someone else happy is more than anyone can bear!

Whenever a person looks to another person to cure or solve their dysfunctions or heal their past hurts it creates tension that retards the process of connection, and threatens the future potential of the relationship! Being married doesn't legitimize or make a woman happy or whole any more than having a baby did in ancient biblical times. Women felt illegitimate and even cursed by the fact of not bearing children though a child still didn't result in a healthy sense of self worth! It is extremely unfortunate that society has tied credibility and value to the institution of marriage and not to the substance and the character of the individuals involved. The world and religious people speak of marriage as if God literally gave marriage as another commandment. They literally offer you respect and applause for being married, never mind your; logic, your heart, or whether you walk in love or not. Notice in society and by society's standards, just about every man given any degree of real power by society has a wife. Think about it; pastors, mayors, generals, councilmen, heads of major corporations, and politicians all have wives, or you better.

It's like society says with a wife, we trust you more, your are better and settled, you have good character, you are less likely to be dishonest, and you evidently have found and understand love, because you're married of course. This bodes well for the religious and traditional argument that marriage equals favor and adds a special blessing to the two involved. To me it sounds more like a co-signer rather than a wife! Somehow being married all by itself lends a person a pass and a load of credibility without proof of any of it! However, none of that could be further from the truth! 8 out of 10 of these power-filled marriages are full of manipulation, infidelity, deceit, and reek of desperation to be free from the pressure of holding up the appearance and façade of happiness. Not to mention the deep sense of loneliness, weakness, and loss of true identity! The reluctant truth about marriage as we know it today is that it is a delusion and a systemic fallacy! Marriage has been proven to be almost everything except blessed, thrilling, and filled with favor if we would be honest. The worst part is we fight so hard to stay and stick with this model of marriage; even in the face of our own self-destruction, still we fight to stay.

Why? Why do we hold onto the things that don't serve us well? Why do we insist that if it worked for them it will work for me? This kind of thinking has ravaged people of faith and the United States generally speaking. We simply are not all the same nor are we created the same! There are better and safer ways to engage in marriage and covenant in a modern and progressive culture.

The Genius Of The Mistress

Before you dismiss the idea of the mistress and her reality, take a step back and don't throw out the baby with the bath water. This talk is not an endorsement of cheating or infidelity by men or women. And it is not a celebration of wayward and insecure women as if they were wise. It is also not an approval of men who say they are committed to one woman, but are still open to other women. However there are some lessons that every girlfriend and wife can learn from the strategies used by the mistress. I believe any women seeking to learn how to have success in relationship can learn her strategies, then add them to herself and strengthen her ability to have a relationship. The mistress is a woman having an extramarital sexual and emotional relationship with a man already dedicated to another women or married. The mistress is an opportunist; her agenda is not to mess up another's relationship because she's jealous. The mistress has just happened upon a man who is responsive and open to her appeal and magnetism for one reason or another.

The main reason the man is responsive to the mistress is that she is the (miss-stress) and fundamentally she causes him to "Miss-Stress". The word genius for our use is a person who has the ability to make the emotional, mental, and relational adjustments without the need for approval of those within their community, family, or social networks. They literally create their own space with a man and disregard the standards of society. The question why are committed men open to the wooing of the mistress, is a question I will attempt to answer for you now. You may be asking the question; what does the mistress know that the wife and girlfriend don't know? What gives the mistress opportunity, position and power over the wife and girlfriend already in a relationship with the man? Does the mistress possess some mysterious knowledge only given to the sidepieces of the world? No, I believe she operates in a strategy or a wisdom that is born out of, paying attention and being a realist. Then it's partly out of her own sense of desperation not that she is actually desperate.

The strategies and wisdom she has discovered I believe can be learned and used very effectively in all of our love relationships. Her genius is not super freakiness nor mind-blowing sex and it's not rocket science either. Her real genius is; her ability to gain, access, influence, and a particular kind of understanding with the man that your in a committed relationship with. Let me address the basic ingredients of her Genius!

- **She is a Realist** – Which is to say she has successfully wrapped her mind around the reality of what she has with this man. Her contentment keeps her from running too far emotionally ahead in the process. She doesn't try to turn the affair into something that it's not! Her earthy rational provokes candor from him. Her balanced approach earns her his trust and communication that ultimately builds a bond between them.

  The mistake that the wife or girlfriend make is, they assume that because they got a signed deal, and are in a relationship with the man, that this automatically is going to give them full access to the man's private parts an the areas of his heart and life, but this is not so! The truth is this access to a man's heart are given in exchange for being; reasonable, rational, and realistic. Not ignoring facts, and not seeking to force her way into the deeper spaces of his life. As a result though you're married to him or committed to him the mistress gets an all access pass to what's really going on in his heart and his life and the man is becoming more and more closed to the wife and girlfriend but opening to the mistress. The wife and girlfriend tend to be very given to societies assumptions about relationships and marriage. These assumptions don't serve them well though. They believe in the ideas so much that they refuse to stop and rework their approach even in the face of failure and loosing the man they are fighting for. While the mistresses' feet are planted on real street, the woman and the wife's feet are planted on the social assumptions that a man has to give you what you believe is due to you based on your position in the man's life, however this is flat out fantasy and not realistic.

- **She Takes The Inch** – The idea of "taking the inch" is metaphoric for the limited amounts of a man's life he starts giving the woman access to in the beginning of a relationship. He may give you an inch of his attention, an inch of his time, or maybe an inch of his private convictions or his worldview. An inch of his background and childhood experiences. He may only share certain portions of what is transpiring in his family's affairs away from you. These layers and compartments within a man's heart and life can be endless. All the while the more you commit to him and like him; the more you will develop a desire to gain access to these areas in order to change them, help him, or to fix them. Regardless of your motivation to access deeper levels of your man, what you are doing is seeking the mile. You have heard the old adage "you give them an inch, and they'll take a mile" Instead of being accepting and patient of where you are in the journey of the relationship.

It begins to appear as force and a disrespect of what has already been "given" to you by the man. You should be spending your energy getting to know him and building his trust in you. Yet it seems you are seeking to take something that he hasn't yet given to you! The man begins to read this behavior however harmless it may be as manipulation. Manipulation is passive aggressive. Meaning it is not overt or obvious yet it is very aggressive, confrontational, and can even become violent. One of the worst things you can do in your relationship ladies is introduce a sense of manipulation to it. Weather it's for your own selfish gain or in your mind for the man's own good! Manipulation will never be respected or appreciated in a relationship by your man! Men hate this and they rebel against it. The mistress in her genius does not seek to access areas of a man's life that she has not been invited into!

She takes what has been offered to her and manages not to fall into the position of manipulation or strong-arming her desire out of the man.

This strategy by the mistress results in a bond, a bond that sponsors a deep sense of trust and companionship between the mistress and the man. This in return causes the man to share his; secrets, ambition, motivations, preferences, wealth, attention, even his fears and weaknesses with the mistress! Both the wife and the mistress start out with an inch, but the wife or girlfriend who appears to be manipulating her way to access, is destined for rejection. The mistress in her genius takes what is available, and takes it with great contentment and pleasantness. As a result she often ends up getting it all! You can dismiss this phenomenon if you want too, but that's not going to bring you success in love relationships. The wife or the girlfriend should work on building his trust in you, then you wouldn't have to spend time prying out of him what the mistress is given freely. The mistress doesn't try to run his business affairs, she doesn't try to dictate how he raises his children, she doesn't argue with him over any of his own personal affairs.

If he asks her for her input she gives it to him. If they disagree she does not take him to task over arbitrary and personal things that or off limits to her. She remains open and supportive through this process whichever way he takes. This is what opens the floodgates for the mistress and causes the man to start telling her more and more and giving her access to his heart without her even asking twice. His appreciation goes up for her; he starts even taking her advice, and believing in her.

All because of her genius behavior he safely trust her and now carries a different respect for her view on various areas of life. Because the mistress isn't "taking it", she ends up getting it all! To be very clear for those women reading this through emotional lenses, the point is not that you should take anything a man dishes out and cherish it, the point is anytime you manipulate or attempt to force a man to give you what you want or need it is likely a disastrous strategy. Your posture and position in your man's life should be; I don't want to take anything you don't desire to give me!

Ladies if you can give it up, you can have it all! Give up force, manipulation, and emotionalism as strategies in your relationships and try taking the inch with a smile!

She Doesn't Desire A Title – The mistress walks in an undeclared nonverbally defined understanding with the man. It is not labeled or hashed out with do's and don'ts. It is organic and altruistic in nature. The relationship or understanding is not meticulously defined but it is very understood between the mistress and the man. Yet, "what" it is; is confirmed almost daily between them without words or a label! This daily interaction produces a strong sense of devotion and respect between them, the kind that would make any wife or girlfriend plunge into jealousy and frustration. Since the mistress doesn't seek a title or a label, society generally likes to insult her. They call her names in an attempt to label her. They say, "she's a secret" this title is meant to be demeaning and a disrespect.

Ultimately, it is a hint and a hinge to her genius because look what keeping a secret can do for you! To covet a title as if the title or label alone gives you power or some special right in a man's life is in my opinion wrong thinking. Titles and labels may give the wife and girlfriend a lot of value and stock in their social circles and on social networks but they carry little to no weight with your true happiness and success in your love relationship. People often mistake the symbol of a thing for the reality of the thing, like the map of a road is not the road itself, nor is the title "wife" actually the happiness, connection, or love you may desire! You can be the "manager" on your job by title but it doesn't make your employees respect you, or give you influence over them. In other words the title or position alone don't give you respect!

You have to communicate your desires with wisdom, respect, and patience. This experience should cause the wife and girlfriend to think about what do I really get with the title and how do I get the substance with or without the title. The record reflects the huge amount of destroyed hearts of women who thought the status of, "in a relationship" on their husband or boyfriends FB page was so good and that the public pictures and declarations meant we made it! But to their shock and awe this did nothing by way of making a man be committed, content, or focused! Regardless of what your opinion of the mistress is, of the way she operates, or the principles that she operates in? Dammit, she gets results! What you believe, think, and what you feel is great if it gets you results, but if you are stressed out about a man who's attention is going in another direction, and what you're doing isn't working? You need to pay attention to the strategies of the mistress.

I call her genius because she's getting easily and freely what you can't get with all of your effort and struggle. I'm saying don't take your position or title with a man and assume anything or take it for granted! If you use these strategies and bring wisdom to the table, your man's response will drastically change. And in his own time he will identify you with a title. Even if its not public at first it will be in principle and ultimately made public, at the perfect time and it will be offered to you with great certainty not for show but because this is what is in the man's heart for you, you'll be genius too!

He That Finds a Wife Made Right

Proverbs 18:22 Says, "He that finds a wife finds a good thing and obtains favor from the Lord."

This scripture has been a stumbling block to many well-intentioned people seeking love and marriage with a desire to do it God's way. This scripture has been customarily and historically interpreted to mean, it is the man's responsibility to search for the woman, and the woman is forbidden to engage or search for the man. This is taught to be how the two can have a; happy, healthy, and blessed union. The wildest thing to me is that I find women often reaffirming and proclaiming this Interpretation with conviction as if there're on to something special by reaffirming it. I find men with less enthusiasm and non-verbally but firmly living up to this notion and even wearing it as a badge of masculinity of some sort. So across the board we accept it and pass it down to the next generation and say, a woman cannot look for a man, but a man must go find the woman.

It is my belief that this interpretation of this scripture is a yoke and a hindrance to the already very challenging idea of love relationships and marriage. In both men and women this interpretation has created angst, anxiety, frustration, and a deep sense of resentment. Women resent the fact of having to sit and wait. To be forced to sit and look good, be dainty, and stand on display like candy or a rack of fruit. Waiting for a man to approach them, comb through them and then decide if he accepts or rejects them! Men share an equally uncomfortable experience bound by this same interpretation. They can never expect a woman interested in them to just come and express their personal interest in getting to know the man. By the time she has put on her dress, done her hair and tried on 10 different pairs of shoes, then shows up flawless only to have to sit and wait for the man to choose her? Then he's got to be funny, win her interest, discern exactly what type of girl she is and do all this by reading her mind? Consequently, both the man and woman are frustrated and both resent the process so much that even if they do get together, they take out their frustration and disappointment on one another.

They say, "I did all this and he's just a regular guy with some issues trying to live." Or, "I did all of that and she's just a regular girl who makes mistakes, has a past and is still learning." Both of them experience disappointment and some regret for allowing this cycle to trick and rob them again. She wanted a king, and he wanted a queen, only to end up with just a girl and a guy. This interpretation that men have to shop for or "find a women" is absurd, men don't even like shopping! The notion that women should be on display is why men tend to try to buy women, as if they are up for sale. Men shouldn't buy women and women shouldn't be for sale. This mentality and belief is destructive and misleading! Both the man and the woman are emotionally exhausted and are victims of a broken unscriptural principle that is completely unproductive. Let me rework the interpretation of Proverbs18: 22 for you. This scripture simply means that a wife is a good thing. If a man finds a woman who is suitable, and willing to be his wife, it "represents" God's favor towards the man! It doesn't mean the man can't be found by the woman or that the man doesn't "represent" God's favor towards the woman.

The emphasis is on discovering a healthy and happy connection between the sexes. It is not on "who" does the finding! Though this verse of scripture started off saying, "He that finds and wife," it was not an explicit command or a revelation of God's perfect will for all relationships. It is love that brings two people together safely, productively, and sensually. It is not the man's ability to chase the woman and seal the deal. You might like the feeling of this distorted belief and thinking, but I'd bet you hate the result of this thinking. If you do like it hang in there but remember you don't get to complain to the rest of us!

Understanding Divorce

Divorce is the premature termination of a marital union between two people, it is evidence of problems deeply seeded within the relationship between the two individuals within the marriage. Divorce catches its bad rap because it is seen as the violator of the union, when in fact it is just the vital sign that the union was suffering, and has finally terminated. It is not my intention to brand divorce as righteous nor unrighteous, it is my attempt to raise our understanding of divorce in the bible, it's relevance and it's role concerning marriages in the modern day. This is my attempt to foster health and healing within individuals and couples who may be suffering or being tormented by the confusion and lack of understanding on the subject of divorce. I am going to be as clear and to the point as I can for the benefit of those of you who have waited so long for a coherent answer on the subject of divorce. One you can understand and an answer that is in concert with the love of God.

Darrell L. Owens

The fist thing one has to understand about divorce is the enormous difference between the culture and meaning which Jesus spoke of when He referenced divorce vs. what we mean and are addressing when we speak on the issue of divorce. The first and glaring fact is when Jesus addresses divorce he is "only" speaking of men divorcing women and never in the slightest way speaking of a woman divorcing a man! This is because at this time if a married woman slept with a man who wasn't her husband it was fornication and adultery, but if a married man slept with another woman who wasn't married he at best took on another wife and at worst just defiled another woman! This is the accurate context and starting point for understanding! Remember that marriage was simply a legally binding contract between the two involved and women were indeed viewed as the man's property. This is important so when you read the scriptures you should keep in mind that "adultery" in the Jewish mentality and Jewish man's mind was about the violation of his property rights to his wife! This was major because individuals didn't have a way of documenting and keeping track of statuses in a reliable way.

Jesus' whole point for reiterating rendering a bill of divorcement and highlighting the status of individuals without this document was to basically prevent crime and to cut out confusion. This was in the wake of men and women who were frivolous and messy concerning their marriages. When Jesus is addressing divorce and adultery His thinking and intent was so far away from our idea of men and women physically cheating on each other! Point of reference, when we speak today about adultery it goes both ways not just adultery on the woman's part. This is fundamentally important to the whole argument. I don't believe you can just take the surface impulse and sense you get from these scriptures and fairly or faithfully apply them to modern culture or marriages today, it's apples and rocks by comparison!

Don't let watered down preaching and slanted teaching bind you to a culture and context that is long gone, to ignore these truths is to not want to get it right! Don't let men try to lock you behind Hebrew and the Greek words translated and changed to fit their views and what they want the bible to say and support.

Remind them that the "culture and context" these scriptures were written in is very well documented also. One of great challenges is the Christian doctrine that teaches the inerrancy of the bible. But let's accept that the bible is inerrant, but then at least let's honestly scrutinize man's interpretation of the bible and ask our is this helpful or even healthy? Mainstream religious leaders are charlatans, they claim to possess accurate spiritual insight and knowledge about others concerning God but they don't, and they are fraudulent! These men and women will quote early religious fathers to support their interpretations while there is another early father at the same time period with the same credibility who says the exact opposite. They then at another instance will quote the early father that disagreed with the other early father on a different subject using only the father and the quote they need to support what they believe.

The first question we have to address is what are the scriptures actually teaching us where we find Jesus mentioning the subjects of divorce, adultery and marriage! Just as a point of reference, the word divorce, in the bible, 85% of the time means to drive away, or to put away, or to separate from!

Let's start with **Malachi 2:16 "For Yahweh God of Israel says That He hates divorce, For it covers one's garment with violence," Says Yahweh of hosts. "Therefore take heed to your spirit, that you do not deal treacherously with the wife of your youth."** The correct context and truth presented here is that Jewish men were mistreating their wives and separating from them for less than honorable reasons and were in fact playing with their minds making them wrong when in fact they did nothing wrong. These men worked in deception and trickery with their own wives. Their dealings were crooked and below board.

Darrell L. Owens

In **Mat 5:31-32 it says, "furthermore it has been said, whoever divorces his wife, let him give her a certificate of divorce. 32 But I say to you that whoever divorces his wife for any reason except sexual immorality causes her to commit adultery; and whoever marries a woman who is divorced commits adultery."** Verse 31 is one of the few verses were the word divorce is found and actually means officially not married or in covenant anymore where divorce follows 'give her a certificate of…" It was the certificate of divorce that rendered the marriage officially over as opposed to just a separation. In these two verses all the other places you find divorce it only means put away or separated. The truth here is, if you divorce your wife officially give her a divorce consisting of a document or certificate of divorce. Secondly, whoever separates from his wife, except for a legitimate substantial reason, causes her to commit adultery! This was because these men in a very male dominated society wanted their cake and to eat it to! Think about how petty a man can be even in today's culture, power hungry and possessive, it was indeed worse in biblical culture. Men would have a woman, defile her, and then leave her caught in the middle.

While he's done with her, he will not allow her to be righteously joined to another man and happy even though he does not want her, sound familiar? This verse is about doing the right thing with people in your life and being fair. It is not a scripture about adultery!

Lets look at **Matt. 19:3-9 "The Pharisees also came to Him, testing Him, and saying to Him, "Is it lawful for a man to divorce his wife for just any reason? 4 And He answered and said to them, "Have you not read that He who made them at the beginning 'made them male and female, 5 and said, 'For this reason a man shall leave his father and mother and be joined to his wife, and the two shall become one flesh 6 So then, they are no longer two but one flesh. Therefore what God has joined together, let not man separate. 7 They said to Him, "Why then did Moses command to give a certificate of divorce, and to put her away? 8 He said to them, "Moses, because of the hardness of your hearts, permitted you to divorce your wives, but from the beginning it was not so. 9 And I say to you, whoever divorces his wife, except for sexual immorality, and marries another, commits adultery; and whoever marries her who is divorced commits adultery.**

Here, if you look at where the Pharisees start off their talk with Jesus it sets the whole context up. "Is it lawful or right for a man to divorce his wife for any reason" this is the point period. Note it says nothing about her divorcing her husband. This verse of scripture is not God offering up his heart on marriage and divorce for today, this is just Jesus addressing the social ills of the day much like we have to do with equal pay for women in the work place or fair policing in the US! In verses 4-5 you find a response from Jesus to these Pharisees and their frivolous inquiry. What Jesus says, Christians again take it out of context and use it to create doctrine and this was not Christ's intent or purpose. Jesus notes specifically the two becoming one flesh, not to infer an inability to separate from each other but to introduce respect and dignity for others and to discourage this "any reason" nonsense these men of this day wanted to use. The two becoming one flesh denotes equality and infers that their covenant existed in and represented unity, any deceit or mistreatment was like lying to your self! Then in verse 6 where Jesus states, "what God has joined together let no man separate" was not Jesus endorsing the notion of "till death do us apart!"

This is a reference to a man coveting another man's wife and disrupting unity or the union of another man's family. Jesus continues on to speak about fornication and adultery warranting divorce or being legitimate reasons for separation and the official end of a Jewish marriage! In verse 7, they ask Jesus, "Why did Moses order us to give a certificate of divorce and to send her away?" Jesus' response was, "because of the hardness of your heart!" Christian leaders immediately assume and teach that this means that the hardness of their hearts was that they just wouldn't obey God's command to stay married once you've been married. Stay in it no matter what, just pray and trust God to change the other's heart. Through abuse, deception, and pain stay married! Stay their even if you need to separate just don't get a divorce! Because God hates you and me getting out of a bad, undesirable, debilitating marriage? He hates us getting a divorce more than anything, or does he just hate for men to abuse their position and power over another's life and happiness? This is the better contextual understanding of what Jesus was saying?

When Jesus says, "From the beginning it was not so" He is not speaking of the beginning of "biblical marriage," because marriage existed before the bible was written or canonized and before ancient language was developed. From the beginning would have to mean when God actually, according to the scriptures introduced connection, sexuality, and comparableness in Genesis meaning the point of connection and union was not to experience a break up. This still doesn't support the notion that God made a law that you should get married and if you do he forbids you to divorce, this is precisely in error and not of God! In verse 9, we see the same heart and spirit Jesus exhibits consistently on the subject that you should not deal treacherously with your wife if your breaking up the unity of the marriage, assuming you got married under the idea of unity. Don't destroy your union or the other person involved recklessly or frivolously, and women should not allow another man to come along and destroy your marital covenant! The way Christians teach and present these scriptures you'd think that Jesus stood up to teach a heavenly doctrinal course on divorce and adultery when this is just not the case.

Jesus merely mentions these subjects while addressing fairness, righteousness, and the deceit within the heart of the religious group of His day.

So this of course leaves us with the question of what do we do when we are confronted with the circumstance of deciding to divorce or not to divorce?

- **Don't Make Divorce about Pleasing God** -This sounds harsh but let's be clear, faith pleases God not whether you are married, divorced, or single! This is one of the great confusions and perversions of faith. Particularly in the Christian faith, when we take everyday decisions and complicate them by saying what does Jesus want me to do? The truth is Christians are to use the light that emanates from our faith to make decisions in our life for the best; then we trust that whatever comes after we have been faithful, God will provide cover, rescue, and grace to endure it all! There is light available to know whether to stay or leave, or to grow up or separate from the wrong marriage partner! When I say light or enlightenment I'm speaking of the; wisdom, knowledge, and truth that flow out of love! If these belong to you, and you respect them, you cannot loose in marriage and love relationships!

- **Love Hard Places** - if you accept the truth about yourself that is self-love. If you accept the truth about others, that is love for those around you. Love is, knowing the truth and accepting that truth without a need to change it, or judge it. Loving yourself and loving the other spouse involved is vital to getting it right when it comes to deciding whether to divorce or not. People have a tendency to try and predict how they are going to feel in the future, these predictions and what if's only serve to make the decision more complicated.

The point of love is to accept the truth not to seek to fashion the truth like a potter does clay or a figurine! In doing this, we miss the whole point of truth and honesty. Misconceptions about God and divorce also trap people in confusion and uncertainty.

Marriage and divorce represent the two most basic human positions any two people can be in, to be together or to be apart. They should be respected as human, temporal, and fragile. They should not be embroiled in human fantasies like movies, plays, and books. Many times there is unity born out of divorce and great separation born out of marriage! Believe what love is telling you about the marriage. Is the conflict or issue in the marriage major or minor to you? Do you accept the spouse's adjustments concerning the issue and more so do you believe the spouses sincerity? At this point in the marriage should you continue in it?

If you listen closely you can hear love answer those questions in your heart! This is not an issue of forgiveness, forgiveness should be a foregone conclusion and forgiveness is not a sign that you should stay! I don't believe in voices in your head, I believe in love and the truth! I believe that the truth speaks and that love has something to say if we want to hear it!

- **If Love Says Stay** - if you want to hear other's opinion that's fine but don't expect them to tell you the way that you should go, that's love's job! If you're going to get it right, silencing the voices of your parents, your friends, your siblings, and your pastor in order to hear love, will be vital! Historically, listening to these people in our lives has been disastrous. If love says stay, even if they say leave, stand your ground. If love says stay don't stop listening to the truth because love will continue to speak and guide the journey you are on. If love says stay be inspired by the potential and opportunity to walk in new normal, provided by love! Continue to grow the marriage, not based on religion, other people, nor, a need to fit in and receive society's approval. Grow it, being fully confident that love has brought you to this point, love will teach you what you need to know and love is having its perfect work in your heart!

- **If love Says Leave** - bow out gracefully, divorce and breaking up in love relationships is never easy because either; you're not taking it well, or they're not taking it well. People in bad marriages and unhealthy relationships stay for different reasons even though they know they need to let go and move on, they feel unable to let go! For some, the attachment to a dysfunctional marriage is full of contradictions in their emotions. Others remain in unhealthy marriages because of physical threat of harm. For others, it's just economic and there are kids involved. Then you have those who have been so emotionally and mentally broken through abuse, they don't have it in them to hear and respond to the call of love in their heart to let go! Regardless of the "why" a person remains in a dysfunctional marriage or relationship it is vitally important that the truth love reveals be acknowledged, accepted and cooperated with! People often ask me, "How do you let go?" I say, you have to "bow out gracefully" not angrily, bitter, or hatefully.

Bowing out gracefully is when you begin to make peaceful, functional, sound decisions that cause dysfunctional people and behaviors to loose their grip in your mind, emotions, and body! Gracefulness minimizes pain and avoids damage, it stifles fear and averts anger. This happens the same way darkness leaves a room when the light is turned on! It is only your unconsciousness and unbelief standing between you and the fresh air of freedom and life again.

Reworked Principles for Marriage

Make and Keep Your Own Marriage Vows - This idea cannot be overstated in a world where systems and powerful people like to dictate and condition the masses to conform as to how something as eclectic as life together should be lived. Start first by dismissing the notion that you are the same as the next couple and growing beyond your need to fit in to a group or section of people that say this is the way! By taking the time out to think through what and whom you are committing to, and what they desire to be committed to them will profoundly change the orientation and dynamics of your relationship. Writing your own marriage vows is an act of declaring your relationship's independence. It will aid in your relationships ability to survive the unique challenges that will present themselves to you both as a couple. At this point if you are considering marriage, the assumption is that you have done due diligence in getting to know the person you are about to make such an enormous life decision with.

The individual's "potential good" is normally on display but at this point there should be some discovery of the "potential negatives" also in this same person. There should be an overwhelming sense of love that accepts them for who and how they are without a need to change or judge. If this part is skipped or if one is assuming they have the right or power to change someone into what they believe they can be, disaster is inevitable! You should be creative with your personal marriage vows, they should reflect insight and compassion towards the one you have developed an intimate love connection with. These vows should be considerate of their desires as well as yours. They should be deliberate, passionate, and in good conscience! We are all too comfortable starting our relationships off with lies like for richer or for poorer. If you haven't really said within yourself that I'd be willing to live forever with you no matter what the circumstance you become poor under, then your telling a lie! Christians don't get to justify a divorce because the man decides not to work and live off of the woman and turn it into an issue of abandonment to legitimize a divorce!

The point is I have limits and I have standards that if crossed will make me reconsider remaining connected to you! What is this writing a blank check and giving a person cart blanche in your life while you stand trapped in something that only destroys you! Don't let deep religious people tell you God will take care of you... ask them since when does God do for me what I can clearly see to do for myself. The scripture says you shall know the truth and the truth shall make you free! The bible literally says it is better not to make a vow at all than to make one and break it! This should all the more highlight the truth of making realistic and honest vows that the two who have to live under them can honestly live with! So, make sure you sit down with you and really get understanding of what you want. Then sit with your potential mate and see what they really want then decide what vows you can make and keep! Vowing to renegotiate the vows periodically is my hint and my frank suggestion for quality assurance!

Embrace The Prenup – a prenuptial agreement is basically what two agree upon from the onset of a marriage covenant. It is designed to set out terms pertaining to the division of land property, the dissolution of assets, and reasonable spousal support in the event of a divorce and break up of the marriage. You typically find these agreements associated with the very wealthy in an attempt to protect their money and assets from being divided or taken. It is a fact that ancient societies used contracts with pre-laid out terms and conditions of marriage covenants. I believe that this strategy should be re-employed today to enhance our current culture and help erect a new model for the marriage covenant in general. The prenuptial agreement will help in a couple of ways first, if a marriage covenant possesses an expiration date and is not renewed then it makes moving on and moving forward clear, concise, and efficient! Clear, concise, and efficient are the very last words anyone in the modern era would use to define a divorce or a break up! The combination of an expiration date and a prenuptial agreement would literally change the narrative from, break up to moving forward!

Enough cannot be said about demystifying the marriage covenant and taking the emotionalism and fantasy out of it in order to allow individuals to make real choices not choices influenced by feeling in small temporary moments! In almost all cases of a relationship breaking down after time has passed, the individuals tend to regret words spoken and actions acted on after they've had time to calm and have allowed emotions to subside. These individuals tend to realize clearly the equal parts played in the break down in communication and understanding. If they had something in place to possibly prevent those experiences they almost always would have chosen it and to act very differently than they did act. Secondly, the prenuptial agreement can be a fair and healthy way to discourage infidelity and mistreatment within the marriage. With the prenuptial agreement one would be able to enact reasonable penalties on the person who violates the union and agreement! It would very different from the lopsided system of judgment we have today that tends to favor the woman in most instances. For example, someone caught cheating, the spouse in good standing could be released immediately upon proof of the infidelity.

The violating spouse would be on the hook to pay a non-negotiable, non-forfeiting payment of $10,000.00 to the spouse in good standing! This is just an example, this would be reasonable and in no way manipulative. No man or woman wants to be held hostage emotionally or otherwise! It may be a matter of the two saying we both keep what we brought to the relationship, but we split 50/50 what we acquired together in the event of a divorce or non-renewal! It may be an occasion when one or both want to exit the covenant early, the prenuptial agreement may have an early out clause or may be vacated by both parties in agreement. The prenuptial agreement is a way two can, in some honorable fashion, move on quickly from the point of separation and divorce and be completely free to live. This all puts teeth in our commitments but no more or less than what we commit to for a house, car, or a credit card, it all ends with you and I being responsible and keeping our word. Over promising and under delivering in relationships emotionally creates great tension in the earth and does great harm to all of us!

Set An Expiration Date On Your Covenant –

I understand that many will disagree with this because of the popular belief among Christians that marriage is supposed to be now and forever. Many of them will fight me to the death to declare this belief. However, not as many will stand on this belief and give themselves too it completely. There are a couple of scriptures Christians use to support this truth which I believe to be non-biblical, that God intends for marriage to be until death do you part. So, lets look at these scriptures and see plainly what they say, and what they don't say. Genesis 2:24 and Matthew 19:5 which both say the same thing, "for this reason a man shall leave his father and mother and be joined to or cleave to his wife, and the two shall become one flesh." First Adam declares it, then Jesus declares it again. Mathew goes on to say what God has joined together let no man separate. These are two scriptures that are primarily used to support the idea that marriage is supposed to be forever! It is perfectly fine if you personally vow to stay married to one person forever but, you can't sign God's signature to that based off of a few misinterpreted scriptures.

When the scripture says in both Genesis 2 and Matthew 19 a man should be joined to his wife and the two shall become one flesh it is speaking of being joined in spiritual unity not in actuality or eternally. When Jesus says what God has joined together let no man separate, again He is not suggesting we are bound eternally, he is addressing the idea of a married man or a single man coveting another man's wife ie. his property! These scripture must be read within the context they were inspired and spoken in. This is what is called an intertextual echo and a reference to the 10th commandment in Exodus 20:17 you shall not covet your neighbors wife. These are the primary and right interpretations of these scriptures. Then you have Romans 7:2 -3 & 1 Corinthians 7:39 where Paul writes that a woman is bound to her husband as long as he is alive. Again this is in the context that a woman was a man's property, he could have another woman, but she could not be with another man, unless she had received a written bill of divorcement from her former husband and been sent out of his house or separated. Then and only then could she go and marry another man.

This is all Paul is saying. Paul was not building nor was he defending some iron spiritual truth that marriage was expected to be forever! You will find those who would go so far as to twist the scripture in 1Corithians 13:7 that says, "love never gives up" could mean God intended marriage to be forever. This is gross and out of line, love is not marriage and marriage and love are two different things. If you follow Christian logic closely you will find, first they seek to lure you into getting married for love and the free sex. Once you're in the marriage and see the truth that marriage and love are two different things they say well you know you did make a vow and it would be very sinful and wrong before God to go back on your vow. Then they tell you, "hang in there your doing it God's way" and if you go any other way you're going to be cursed and in sin! My point is we are not doing God, the Christian faith, or the millions of well intentioned people caught in the confusion of men's interpretations any good by continuing down this road of beliefs about God's will being marriage forever and until death do you part. The best way forward would be for modern couples to set an expiration date on their marriage covenant.

The marriage can be renewed periodically every 3, 5, or 10 years. Each couple may choose different amounts of time before renewal. The important part is adding in the option to discontinue the relationship honorably and civilized! This idea brings with it; fairness, safety, honesty, freedom, and love in ways the current model will never produce! We seem to be ok just hoping people will be fair and treat each other civilized during a beak down or a break up! This model brings fairness because, it requires the couple to have a prenup and to make clear what they both desire to happen concerning affairs, possessions, and children in the event the marriage covenant is broken or is not renewed. It brings honesty and safety because it encourages truthfulness and stimulates choice. People are people, it doesn't matter what age, stage or level of education one has if pressured in the right way, by the right people at the right time we all are conditioned to capitulate and give in to the strong tide of social pressures to be unfair and selfish. As we all well know, the social morals of the past don't represent the truth of the people of today, they often represent the truth of a people and a culture that is no more.

We also realize that there is grave danger hidden in the heart of a person who feels restricted from being honest about their truth! The truth of how they feel, the truth of what they want, and the truth of what they choose next. It is not safe to live and dwell with person in this state of mind. The expiration date on a covenant also brings freedom and love, because once a person has been freed to embrace their own truth and not suppress it. Once they have been allowed to choose what they actually desire without judgment or manipulation, this sets the stage for true and real love to exist and this can produce wholeness. Each person involved gets an opportunity to accept their own selves and their own truth. Then they can accept the other's truth and personal desires going forward. This is true love and true freedom! Minus the burden of religious manipulation and force to stay or leave!

Have The Ceremony After – The ceremony and reception should symbolize and celebrate accomplishment and success! As it stands the ceremony and reception are celebrations of the attempt at being committed, connected, and cooperative. We spend thousands of dollars on celebrating the marriage in theory not in application! Why not save that expense and that experience for afterwards? After you've proven something not to God, not to the world, and not to your haters, but to yourselves! After you have experienced the challenge of navigating another person's desires, convictions, and temperament. After you have survived at least one cycle of a marriage and covenant and are now ready to renew it willingly and with joy? This is precisely the right time to plan to spend lots of money on something significant not frivolous. This is the time to celebrate and fly in relatives and friends to help you acknowledge your success and commitment and honor for one another. In the light of so much failure with the covenant of marriage why not wait and build strong and then after you know it's real and true, now celebrate your actual greatness rather than your potential success.

Inspiration for Love ReWorked

It was the work of Jason Fried and David Heinemeier and their team at 37signals who compiled a masterful book entitled "REWORK." This was a book about doing business differently. The fundamental lesson it taught was, easy is a better approach to getting things accomplished. The lessons of "Rework" brought an immediate impact to my imagination, creativity, and my perspective on work and ethics. It is one of the clearest and most concise books I have ever read on any discipline. This book changed me in such a way that its title became the way I would frame and articulate my new ideas and new ways of approaching love and relationships. This title also became the way I would articulate a whole emerging and transformative community I call ReWorked Nation. The book "Love ReWorked" will always be in some way an honor to the exceptional work of the team at 37signals. I will forever be thankful, often inspired, and eternally filled with ideas because of this masterpiece.

www.37signals.com/rework

Biography

Pastor Darrell Owens is a man of God with a passion for the genuine faith and consciousness of every man. He is an accomplished thought leader, teacher, and trailblazer for social change and the new generation. Presently he serves as the visionary and Pastor of Sacred Place Community Church at the Union located in the suburbs of Clinton, Maryland where he guides multiple generations that have entered into new conversations with God. He delivers the word of God in a unique, new, clear, and thought provoking way. He rejects legalism, denominationalism, anything not evolving, exclusive and without power to transform.

As an extension of his ministry and passion he is the visionary and creative mind behind the emerging and transformative lifestylebrand – *Reworked Nation*. Reworked Nation is a social change movement.

Through it's efforts he attempts to re-divide, re-interpret, and re-present old images and models that don't serve us well, through better images and more agile models that bring success. He is also the host of Reworked Radio, a daily solution radio show where he provides guidance and insight on everyday issues concerning love, sex, faith,God, and everything taboo. Pastor Darrell is a sought after speaker and counselor. Pastor Darrell is a regular speaker and mentor for boys aged 15-18 at the DC Jail and Dept. of Corrections in Washington DC. He provides support and mentoring to multiple publicschools to motivate young people all around the DMV. He has conducted graduations and the commencement ceremonies for multiple Schools of Religion,Theology & Seminaries. He was bestowed a Honorary Doctorate Degree in Christian Counseling and Theology from the Cornerstone Christian University in Orlando Florida in 2012.

He presently sits on the local board of the Gospel

Heritage foundation. Which sponsors and host the annual

celebration of Gospel at the Kennedy Center each year.

Pastor Darrell was keynote speaker for the National

Chapter of the NAACP at Gettysburg College in

Gettysburg Pennsylvania in 2013.

He has taken his captivating and unconventional brand to

mainstream media as a regular contributing writer with

in Kingdom Voices Magazine Online. Pastor Darrell is

well noted for his extensive work in the area of love,

sexuality, and relationships. Here he works to rebuild

destroyed trust, and present new ideals for interpreting

love and relationship through the lens of modern culture

and Christ Consciousness.

Pastor Darrell's mantra is, *"Somebody Can Win with The*

Hand That You are Losing With." He doesn't just suggest

greatness...he insists on it!

Connect with Darrell Owens Socially

www.iamdarrellowens.com

FB @iamdarrellowens

TW @iamdarrellowens

IG @iamdarrellowens

Please send any questions that this book has sponsored but you feel did not answer for you, to:

iamdarrellownes@gmail.com

Darrell L. Owens

Published in the United States by iamdarrellowens networks/publishing

For information about booking Darrell Owens for lectures, panel
discussions or for special discounts for bulk purchases please contact
iamdarrellowens.com or call 240-778-7707

Cover Design & Interior Design by Latoya A. Benson & IV
Professionals Consulting
www.latoyabenson.com

Cover Photo by Aisha Lateefah Wise

Sr. Editor – Denise A. Vinson for The Vinson Group Inc.
Editing – Heather L. Owens for Avery's Aim Productions
Editing – Latoya A. Benson for IV Professionals Consulting

All scripture quotations are from The Holy Bible
King James Public Domain
New King James Copyright 1979, 1980, 1982 Thomas Nelson
New American Standard Copyright 1960, 1962, 1963, 1968, 1971,
1972, 1973, 1975, 1977, 1995 Lockman Foundation

ISBN: **978-0692493182**
Printed in The United States of America